THE CHRISTIAN DOCTRINE OF HISTORY

THE CHRISTIAN DOCTRINE

OF HISTORY

JOHN McINTYRE

M.A., B.D., D.LITT.

PROFESSOR OF DIVINITY, UNIVERSITY OF EDINBURGH

OLIVER AND BOYD

EDINBURGH: TWEEDDALE COURT

LONDON: 39A WELBECK STREET, W. 1

FIRST PUBLISHED . . . 1957

COPYRIGHT © 1957 JOHN McINTYRE

PRINTED IN GREAT BRITAIN BY
OLIVER AND BOYD LTD., EDINBURGH

PREFACE

CERTAIN sections of the material presented in this book were prepared for lectures delivered in 1953 in Union Theological Seminary under the Fulbright Scheme for the Exchange of Scholars. Most grateful acknowledgment is made, therefore, to the Fulbright Electors who control the Scheme, and to the President of the Seminary, Dr Pitney Van Dusen, for the warm welcome which he gave to one who was at that time a representative of the Australian academic world. It would be remiss of me to fail to mention the many discussions which I had with Dr Reinhold Niebuhr during that visit, evidence of which will not be lacking in the pages that follow.

In its final form, the material was presented in 1956 as lectures to the Faculty of Divinity of the University of Otago. The kindly hospitality extended to me by Principal John Allen, by Professor G. A. F. Knight and the other members of the Faculty, and by the Rev. James Mathieson of Knox Church, Dunedin, remains a vivid memory.

JOHN MCINTYRE

EDINBURGH

1957

CONTENTS

CHAPTER ONE

HISTORY AND DOCTRINE

THE perennial task of the Church, to which she was commissioned by Her Lord Himself, is the communication of the Gospel; and to this end she has had to employ concepts which did not belong to "the given" of Revelation, or yet to the written record of Revelation. Sometimes these concepts have been drawn from the culture, the society, the economy of her contemporaries; and on occasion the concepts she has employed have not been adequate to the responsibility she sought to impose upon them, with resultant heresies. Sometimes the concepts have been drawn from a previous age, and literalism, fundamentalism, and even a false orthodoxy, have prevented men from hearing the Word of Life. Despite these dangers, the Church's duty has remained, for communication takes place in no other way, except through the hearing and understanding of the Word.

At this point, the second responsibility of the Church emerges, though it is no new or other responsibility but is in fact the converse of the first. It is her theological responsibility of testing the concepts in which the Word has been expressed, by the criterion of "the given" of Revelation, to discover whether what has been said is that "which must be said under all circumstances" or that "which may not be said under any circumstances". (Karl Barth, *The Doctrine of the Word of God*, 1/1, E.T., p. 88.)

In fulfilling this responsibility, theology has in every age endeavoured to construct as coherent an account as possible of this conceptual interpretation of the Christian faith, in the form of a dogmatic science; and however elaborate or simple the science may be, the ultimate justification for it lies in the extent to which it has remained in organic union with "the given" of Revelation and the record of Revelation, and has consequently assisted in the faithful communication of the Gospel to the contemporary generation. Cut loose from such organic union, it drifts into arid scholasticism and becomes science for science's sake, interesting after the fashion of cross-word puzzles but in the end self-frustrating.

As the Church has conducted this task of examining and clarifying the concepts in which the faith is from time to time expressed, certain important facts have emerged.

(1) The first is that what has appeared to one generation to belong to the essentially "given" has not been accepted as being so by other generations. The unsearchable riches of the Gospel of Jesus Christ have been exhibited in the history of the Church across the centuries in a whole variety of forms. The ever present temptation before the Church is to accept any one of these forms as permanent, after it has in reality become an incommunicable, that is, after it has ceased to bring men and women into living encounter with God through Jesus Christ. On the other hand it is constantly difficult for each generation to realise that the vehicles which it finds most adequate for kerugmatic and didactic expression do not themselves belong to the "given-ness" of the Gospel.

Two contemporary examples may illustrate this point. First, while we are today well aware that the doctrine of the Trinity does not belong to the "given" which the Bible records, or to the original situation of the Incarnation, it comes as a shock to us to realise that the concept of "Revelation" is not in that category either. Not only did the Church for many centuries find it possible to describe what happened when "the Word was made Flesh and dwelt among us", without using this term, but further, because of the history of theology in the last hundred years or so, the term "Revelation" has acquired a significance for us which it has never had in the whole history of the Church. But it is extremely difficult for us to become completely aware of this fact, since both our contemporary studies of the history of dogma and even many of our exegetical commentaries upon the scriptures are influenced by the prevalence of the concept of "Revelation". Indeed, one of the chief but little recognised problems of Christology today is that of how a Christology which employs "Revelation" as its regulative concept is related to the Chalcedonian Christology with its hypostatic union of two natures.

The second example I have chosen is that of the idea of history. It is now a theological commonplace to emphasise the fact that Christianity is a historical religion. In this vein we hear such statements as : "God acts in history", "God reveals Himself in history", "The Incarnation is the centre of history", and so on. The idea of history and ideas about history enter into most present day analyses of the nature of God, into most interpretations of the person and work of Jesus Christ and into almost all accounts of the theology of the Old Testament or of the New Testament, that is, into almost all of what is called "Biblical Theology". What is not always realised is that historical conceptions of this sort are unique to our time; that because of developments not only in theological thought concerning the subjects peculiar to itself but also in the fields of historical methodology and of the critique of historiography, our understanding and our interpretation of the historical element in the Christian faith are not the same as those of any previous generation.

These developments both within and outside theological thought are of such importance that a detailed mention of some of them will further establish the main contention. For example:

(a) It is only within the last fifty years that there has been any serious and general questioning of the historicity of the Gospel narratives from within the Christian Church. For many centuries it had been accepted that the events of the Life, Death and Resurrection of Our Lord were as the Gospels described them, but questioning of the historicity elicited new appreciation of what the Gospels were really intended to do and a new appreciation of what history really is. Such an examination led inevitably to a new definition of the relation of the great facts of the faith to history—definition which was impossible in terms of the old acceptance of the historicity of those events that are central to Christian belief.

(b) The tumultuous episodes of the twentieth century have compelled ministers of the Gospel to relate their message to the history of our day. This responsibility has sharpened our insight into riches of the Gospel which were undreamt of in the midst of the Victorian optimism. Men have asked questions concerning the nature and purpose and final end of history, and answers have been sought in the content of the Christian Gospel. It is significant that when O. Cullmann in endeavouring to explain the relation of Christ's First Coming to His Second Coming should employ the 1944-45 analogy of D-day and V-day.

(c) Strictly within theology itself, other influences have been at work to make us more conscious than any of our predecessors of the relation of the events of the faith to history. For example, the greatest figure of the nineteenth century to influence the twentieth is generally recognised by Protestant theologians to be Kierkegaard. Now at the heart of his teaching there is a scepticism (most noticeable in the *Unscientific Postscript*) concerning history, so profound that he regards all knowledge of the historical as problematical. Those who have not been influenced by him to the extent of accepting all his doctrine as of another apostle born out of due season, have nevertheless been so seriously affected by his work as to revise all their conceptions of history and of the historicity of the events of the Gospel. Even when they take flight into *Heilsgeschichte* as an escape from the ambiguity of the other kind of history, they all too obviously indicate their concern about the very issue which Kierkegaard raised. Historical scepticism was enunciated as early as 1929 by Paul Tillich in *An Interpretation of History* (p. 264): "The Christological question is the question of Christ as the centre of history. This question is entirely independent of the problems of historical enquiry into the facts behind the rise of the Biblical picture of Christ. The exposition of these facts can only lend probability—and with respect to the historical Jesus, a very faint probability."

Such scepticism has forced theologians to revise accepted standards of historical fact and probability in relation to the Gospel events. In latter days the whole problem has become acute with the development from the form-critical methods of Biblical analysis to a full-blown demythologisation of what was regarded in previous days as the very content of the faith itself.

(d) The prevalence of the Marxist interpretation of history, arising as it did from the very heart of Judaistic Messianism and apocalypticism and achieving popularity with those who had lost confidence in the idea of progress, has compelled Christian thinkers to revise their ideas on history. This compulsion has become the more urgent as Marxism has grown from a philosophy into a possible way of life and an active political force competing with Western civilisation and democracy for the allegiance of millions of human beings. With false views of the meaning and end of history expressed on many sides, it is inevitable that the Church should offer to men the Christian account of these matters; and should, in historical concepts, find a successful vehicle of communication of the facts of the faith.

(e) In this generation, too, historians have become acutely aware of the problem of methodology, and of the presuppositions which, often unconsciously, affect their historical evaluations and prevent impartial judgment. The subjective position of the writer, whether it be economic, social or national, is now openly recognised as an influence in the historical judgments that he makes—but an influence which is no longer taken to invalidate those judgments, as it would have been said to do in a period when the scientific objective attitude was thought to be the norm of historical statement. The historicity of the events associated with the Incarnation, which was in the past widely questioned because it was recognised to be dependent upon the "faith" of the Christian historian, comes up for fresh analysis and assessment in the light of the contemporary revision of the canons of historicity. Whereas a previous generation of theologians made light of the historical nature of the central events of the faith, and because of their embarrassment endeavoured to speak of the eternal values of Christianity, the modern insistence has been upon the historicity of the Gospel records and of the faith there recorded.

Each of these considerations—and the list is by no means exhaustive—is so important in our time that today we approach the question of the relation of Christianity to history from a position unprecedented in the history of the Church.

For that reason, what we regard as the Biblical view of time or history can only by an anachronism be said to be that of the Biblical writers themselves; yet that is exactly the anachronism of which so many of our contemporaries are guilty. For instance, to say, as O. Cullmann does, that Christ is the centre of linear history is to say something which the New Testament writers would never have said in just that way; in other words, it is to say something which does not belong to the "given" of which the Evangelist spoke when he said that "the Word was made flesh" but which is often taken by many writers of our day to do so.

But to make this statement is to speak legitimately, for our generation has found historical thought to be one of the most intelligible vehicles of the Christian faith. If previous generations have used the Aristotelean metaphysic, or more recently scientific concepts, not only for apologetic but also for dogmatic purposes, then we have turned to history and historical concepts for these same purposes. Even when other concepts, such as Revelation or myth or *Kairos*, are employed in dogmatic exposition, there almost always appears some reference to a historical framework or some conception of history. Our immediate task, therefore, is to examine the implications of this contemporary use of historical concepts in dogmatic formulations.

(2) A second important fact has emerged from our awareness of the use which the Church makes of concepts and ideas which do not exactly belong to the "given" of Revelation. It is this, that these concepts in their new reference acquire meanings which they did not have apart from this application. Professor John Baillie has, in discussions, frequently demonstrated a similar point, with the illustration of the use of the term "Father" as a description of God. Before it was thus used, the term "Father" had a certain connotation which would include such notions as physical progenitor, head of the family, member of the household with unique economic responsibilities, a person who could be expected to have certain kindly feelings towards the members of his family, and so on. When the term is applied to God, and particularly to the God and Father of our Lord Jesus Christ, then at once it becomes obvious that not all of these previously enumerated characteristics can be applied to God, *simpliciter*, and that in fact some must be omitted. Such notions as all-providing care, willingness

to suffer in the bitterest sufferings of His children, loving in spite of their sinfulness and unlovableness, loving to the point of giving His own Son to die in agony—these now become predominant. This new conception of Fatherhood now becomes the norm of all fatherhood; it becomes the "primary" meaning of the term, and human fatherhood the "secondary" meaning. The situation may be represented symbolically. If prior to its application to God the idea of fatherhood is defined as connoting $a\ b\ c\ d\ e$, then this idea is accepted, humanly speaking, as applicable to God because of the presence of elements $a\ b\ c$—more applicable, for example, than the idea of being a High Tower, which is definable as $p\ q\ r$. Elements $d\ e$ are omitted, but for them are substituted in the Divine reference elements $f\ g\ h$. But since they have been put into this new context $a\ b\ c$ do not remain quite what they were in connection with $d\ e$—for example, the care that God has for His children, His love which goes to the uttermost, far transcend anything of which a human father is capable. It would be perhaps a more adequate symbolism to say that Divine Fatherhood is definable as $A\ B\ C\ F\ G\ H$.

If, then, it is true that such a notion as that of "Fatherhood" is so radically transformed by its relation to the Revelation of God in Jesus Christ, it is equally true that those other concepts of which we have been thinking, which do not belong so integrally to the "given" of the Gospel, are profoundly affected by their new sphere of reference. The very word "Revelation", which had been and has been used in other connections, acquires its primary meaning as the description of what happened when "the Word was made flesh"—so much so that the question has been asked whether this is not its only meaning. Even if we are not prepared to give the affirmative answer, nevertheless the fact that the question can be asked is evidence of the way in which concepts are changed by being brought into relation with the events of the Incarnation. So, too, the idea of history has been affected in just this way. When it becomes a vehicle of expression of the contents of the Christian Gospel it may, indeed it must, retain some of the elements which it had previously. But we state less than the true case if we do not also maintain that it acquires new significance.

To examine the relation of these newer significances to the old is yet a further part of our purpose in this study.

The consequence which seems immediately to follow from this situation is that, provided these new significances are of sufficient importance, we may then legitimately formulate a Christian doctrine of any one of the concepts in question. The many new things which are being said in our time concerning history in its relation to the Revelation of God in Jesus Christ—they have formed the dominant themes in British and American theology if not also in Continental theology since World War II—suggest that the time has come for the more concise definition of what we may call "the Christian doctrine of history". Such definition would not involve the invention of some new thing which has not existed before we embarked on the task, but would rather involve the crystallising of ideas that are to be found throughout most contemporary theology, both explicitly stated and implicitly presupposed. This doctrine would be a natural and necessary corollary to the Christian doctrine of man, but it would differ on the one hand from such a doctrine in that it would take fuller account of the ways in which human activities are related to each other across the time span, and from the Christian doctrine of society in that it would allow for the ways in which individuals act within communities and for the importance of human volition as against organised change in developments from one generation to another, and be less concerned with the structural analysis of the form of society in different generations.

Now the Christian doctrine of history is not merely a *Heilsgeschichte*, a recitation of the events that constitute the economy of salvation, a rehearsal of the mighty acts by which God has accomplished the redemption of His creatures. It will be expected to include many references to these mighty acts; it may even say that these mighty acts determine the quality of history; but in so far as history involves human activity as well as the Divine, an account of what God has done in history cannot exhaust our description of history. In fact, one of the major problems which we shall have to face is how what is called *Heilsgeschichte* is related to ordinary history— and whether it forms a separate continuous line in distinction from the latter ; whether it is, on the contrary, interwoven with the latter; and finally, if it is so, how we are to describe those portions of ordinary history which coincide with *Heilsgeschichte*.

But just because it is a *Christian* doctrine of history, it will be a doctrine which is in organic union with the whole corpus of the Christian faith. There is nothing exceptional in this situation, for so it has always been in the history of Christian doctrine. The doctrines of the Church are not a set of propositions isolated from one another, each establishing and maintaining itself in intellectual independence of the others. They form a unity, and the statement or defence of any of them draws upon the others. For reasons of heresy arising within the Church or of calculated attack from without, interest may shift from point to point within this unity. In one century the nature of the Three-in-Oneness of God may be the subject of particular examination; in another, the Person of Jesus Christ; in yet another, the place of grace in the Sacraments; in modern times the doctrine of Creation, the sinlessness of Jesus Christ, and so on ; but on each of these occasions and at each of these points the whole body of Christian belief was involved and had to be drawn upon for the elaboration of any single one of the doctrines. The Christian doctrine of history (which in our time has come up for consideration for the reasons, already discussed, operating both outside and inside the Church) will exhibit that same sort of dependence upon the rest of Christian doctrine and that same readiness to draw upon the latter for its fullest development and statement.

Of course, to speak of a Christian doctrine of history is to run the risk of the fiercest attack from the technical historians, who regard this as their own special field. If Toynbee's presentation of history can earn for him the sharpest criticism from fellow historians, what shall be the fate of theologians who venture into the same arena? The objection is serious, and it has to be considered, but it is by no means final. The objection could, I believe, be sustained on three conditions: first, if the exponent of the Christian doctrine of history denied completely the validity of what the technical historians were doing; secondly, if, consequent to such denial, he endeavoured

B

to do what they were doing but in some manner which he imagined to be better; thirdly, if he could not, in some way at least, show the relevance of what the technical historians were doing to the Christian doctrine of history, or in some way describe the connection of the two. The affirmation of these conditions carries this immediate consequence that the technical historian on his part will be expected to wait to hear out the exponent of the Christian doctrine, and not on *a priori* grounds deny that such a doctrine is possible. The Christian exponent, on his part, would be unwise not to honour these conditions, at least as sound working principles. If he finds after employing them for some time that he cannot continue to accept them, then the problem which he will be required to face is whether the fault lies with himself or with the technical historian.

But such an issue ought to be raised late in the day and not at the outset of his exposition. In any case, the fact that specialists, without necessarily having Christian presuppositions, are working in any given field is not in itself sufficient ground for the denial of the possibility or yet of the validity of a Christian judgment on the subject matter of that enquiry. The existence of many secular anthropologists is not in itself a deterrent from the formulation of a Christian anthropology; indeed, it could well be regarded as making the latter more necessary. A Christian sociology, a Christian analysis of the laws that govern social groupings and developments of social standards and conventions, is as valid a subject for exposition as, say, a Marxist sociology. While there may not be a Christian physics, there is at least a Christian conception of the nature of matter, as the late Archbishop Temple reminded us in his references to "Christian materialism" and as Dr. George MacLeod has so frequently affirmed in *We Shall Rebuild* and in other publications. Therefore it is no cause for surprise if the Christian faith, which affirms that "man's chief end is to glorify God and enjoy Him for ever", should include a doctrine of history, which, however much more precisely we shall come to define it later, is at least concerned with man's activities in relation to his fellow men.

It is generally assumed that this emphasis on the historical quality of the Christian religion commits Christians to a quite

unique view of the nature of the God who has thus acted in
relation to history. No unmoved Mover of the spheres, this;
no *Deus Absconditus*; no concatenation of bloodless categories.
All of this is perfectly correct, and cannot be repeated too
frequently even today, for the temptation to de-historicise
theological thinking appears still to be a real one, both for
those who endeavour to translate God's historical activity into
metaphysical process and for those who practise de-mytho-
logisation as a means of avoiding some of the difficulties caused
by a literal concern with God's action in history.

But it has not been so commonly realised that this conviction of the rootedness of Christianity in history commits
the Christian exponent to a quite specific doctrine of history.
Just as God by His many actions in history, and supremely
in the Revelation of Himself in a life that was lived, in a death
that took place on earth, and in a Resurrection that came as the
culmination and the vindication of all that had previously
happened, in certain specifiable places and in definite historical
times transformed all men's previous views of Himself, so by
these very deeds He transformed not only their views of
history but also history itself. It is easy to see that God's
revelation of Himself to man, and His redemption of him in the
course of history, are the basis of a quite specific anthropology.
But the implications for historical analysis have not been so
swiftly and surely followed up. The impression too often given
is that history is something in which things happen, a structure
in which the events of Revelation and Redemption take place,
a framework relatively unaffected by the actions of God and
man that occur within it. The further suggestion is often made
that while history is the same for all men, their differences of
opinion about it occur at the level of "interpretation" and do not
affect the inner nature of the historical process. The purpose
of this present study is to demonstrate that the Christian,
because of his belief in God's Revelation of Himself in history,
is committed to a unique doctrine of history; that this doctrine
is not merely a theory concerning facts which are accepted by
all men, but relates to the central nature of history itself.

As we turn, therefore, to the discussion of the Christian
doctrine of history, we must keep in mind certain considerations.

The first is that the very word "history" does not mean the same thing to every person; nor is it as easily identifiable as, say, the planet Venus. It might be said that there are as many views of history as there are of man, except that the situation is still more complex, since people who hold similar views of man may hold varying views of history. Part, then, of our task in stating the Christian doctrine of history is to make plain what we mean by history, as well as to expound what history means, which latter task has often been regarded as the total content of the doctrine. Secondly, we have to recognise that because the idea of history and historical concepts are the vehicle of religious and theological expression, they have been affected by this reference. We cannot expect, therefore, to have an idea of history which is equally acceptable to believers and unbelievers. Thirdly, in our account of the doctrine of history, we shall be obliged to present it in relation to the whole corpus of Christian belief; and its validity will ultimately stand or fall with that corpus. Fourthly, we embark upon exposition of the doctrine in the realisation that the testing and clarification of it is one of the Church's inescapable tasks, for it is necessitated by the fact that the idea of history and historical concepts are now being constantly used in the Church's proclamation, in her political and socio-economic judgments, and in her dogmatic formulations.

CHAPTER TWO

HISTORY AND DEFINITION

ONCE it is affirmed that the Christian Revelation commits the believer to a Christian doctrine of history, then immediately there arises a responsibility to say what that doctrine is. I propose to come to terms with this responsibility by offering, to begin with, a definition of history. Such a definition, it is hoped, will not only enable other investigators in the field to know just what the Christian conception is, but will also enable us to understand more fully what is and what is not comprehended within the limits of the Christian doctrine. It is not, however, intended that the definition will be self-evident, in the way in which it is sometimes assumed that certain mathematical definitions are, for, even in mathematics, the day of the self-evident definition is past. The definition is offered in the belief that its justification will lie in the kind of exposition that it will enable us to construct and in the kind of conclusions that it will assist us to reach. It is not suggested that the validity of the conclusions will consist in their logical agreement with the premises, for the definition does not have that sort of logical priority to the conclusions. In fact, the situation is that definition, exposition and conclusions are all in the same position and are submitted together and as a whole for consideration as the way in which the Christian looks at history. In any case, self-evidence is a completely relative concept, relative, that is, to the realm of discourse in which the proposition of which it is affirmed occurs. It does not exist in what we might call any "atomic" form in isolated propositions.

Our proposed definition is as follows: history is meaningful occurrence, and more particularly occurrence the meaning of which is a construct out of certain categories, namely, Necessity, Providence, Incarnation, Freedom and Memory. Naturally such a definition immediately calls for some fuller account of what is meant by each of these categories, but before we proceed to this task, it is necessary first of all to make certain comments about the definition as a whole and the less specific elements in it:

(1) The definition seeks to emphasise the fact that history is not the totality of occurrence, all the events in the created order. For example, it is conceivable that certain events are at this moment taking place on the other side of the moon, that similar events have taken place often in the past, and that they therefore occupy a place in the space-time continuum. But since it is by only a very long chain of cause and effect that they can be related to events describable in terms of the enumerated categories, or have any significant connection with them, they cannot be regarded as "historical". Nor is history all meaningful occurrence, for in pre-history, in geological process and in the lowest stages of plant and animal evolution, there is meaningful occurrence of a kind, yet though it may exhibit structural patterning or purposeful development, the entities involved are not of the sort to which all the categories mentioned could precisely be ascribed. To them, in fact, some of the categories might be applied, such as, for instance, necessity or Providence, but since others are not applicable, those occurrences in which these entities participate are not of a strictly historical nature. It is only when all of the categories are present and operative that historical occurrence takes place.

(2) Miss Susan Stebbing once said that "the words 'meaning' and 'means' have both harmful and systematic ambiguity" (*A Modern Introduction to Logic*, p. 499). This criticism is never so pertinent as when it is directed against the use of these words in connection with history. It is most important, therefore, to indicate exactly what is intended by this potentially misleading word in the definition we are now considering. When it is affirmed that historical occurrences are those occurrences the meaning of which is a construct out of the various categories listed, what we are saying may be conveyed by the following propositions. First, that historical occurrences require for their adequate description the employment of certain categories; that is, that historical occurrences can be properly described only in terms of these specified categories. Secondly, that historical occurrences imply for their actual existence

these same categories; and that the categories here come together in a unique way to produce something that is *sui generis*, something that is quite different from necessary occurrence in the naturo-physical realm, from logical implication and from processes within the Godhead, such as the generation of the Son by the Father. So, when we say that "the meaning of *x* (historical occurrence) is *a b c d* (a construct out of the various categories)", we are in effect saying both that *x* is defined by description and that *x* is defined by stating the conditions of its possible occurrence.

There is, I believe, no need to apologise for the realist epistemology that lies at the back of this definition of history; for while Hegel and the Hegelians hold the principle that "the real is the rational" to construct their Absolute Idealism, it is also permissible to interpret this principle in the reverse way to theirs, and to affirm that "the rational is the real". Then we are maintaining that the relations which we affirm between objects are not mental connections invented by us to co-ordinate a world (in itself atomic), but are in fact the connections which do exist "out there". The conditions under which we apprehend reality are the conditions under which reality exists. Once it is admitted that the mind knows only ideas and relation between ideas, then the Cartesian bifurcation so much deplored by Whitehead and Berdyaev for reasons so diverse, becomes inevitable. When we think about things and their relations to each other, we think about real things and real relations, and not about ideas of them which we somehow have "in our minds". Otherwise knowing would become a relation between mind and itself, and would be ultimately self-frustrating. Nor is it satisfactory to say in terms of Vaihinger's refinement of Kantian epistemology that we think of things *als ob*, as if, they were related in the way in which our mind thinks them to be: to hold such a view is to remain bounded within the confines of the Idealist theory of knowledge.

An emphasis upon such realism is a very necessary part of the Christian doctrine of history, for the Christian surrenders his birthright the moment he allows himself to renounce the view that his is not just another "interpretation" of a set of objective facts which can be scientifically determined by impartial observers in the field. That is, he must hold to *both* elements in his definition of history, saying not only that his definition is a description which enables men to distinguish history from all the other occurrences that take place in the created order or beyond it, but also that his definition states the conditions which are necessary for its actual occurrence. We shall later be concerned with interpretation and history, but for the present we shall say that the Christian may find himself obliged to hold that for him the so-called "facts" are different from what they are for the unbeliever.

For what in effect is here being affirmed is that history requires its own metaphysic. History will always remain an insoluble problem for a metaphysic which conceives of reality as an ideal realm of essences (idealism) or as a series of sense-data (empiricism). Worse still, history will remain indescribable in terms of such systems, so that the very problem of history cannot be formulated by them. The failure of philosophy to deal on the whole adequately with history has been due not simply to the fact that it had a wrong idea of time, or that history deals with particulars and philosophy with universals, or even that the irrationality of history cannot be confined within the limits of any coherent philosophy; rather has this failure been due to the fact that philosophy has not realised that history is a unique occurrence in the universe, that it cannot be resolved into something other than itself, and that consequently it requires a metaphysic of its own. That which was formulated in times when the ontological status of sense-data, or the nature of logical analysis, or, for that matter, the subtleties of semantics were thought to be the major problems of philosophy, can scarcely be expected *a priori* to have immediate relevance to, or be sufficiently comprehensive to explain, the profounder problem either of the knowledge of other selves or of the nature and knowledge of history. In fact, it would prove rather an interesting task to write the history of philosophy showing how the metaphysical preconceptions of philosophers had prevented them not only from stating the true nature of certain subjects within the real world but also from realising the problems attendant on these subjects. The history of philosophical treatment of the existence and nature of God would illustrate the former of these two points and that of the nature of our knowledge of other selves the latter. Our immediate contention, however, is not predominantly philosophical, though it has philosophical and metaphysical implications; it is simply that the Christian believes that the terms in which he apprehends and interprets history are descriptions of what history really is and of how it takes place.

It is for this reason that the word "categories" has been used rather than "concepts" to designate the constitutive elements of history. The word "concept" would almost imply that these elements were peculiarly mental in character, and that they might or might not correspond to real existents, ideal constructions found to be useful in the rationalising and making coherent of material which in itself is a "big buzzing blooming confusion". The word "category", on the other hand, while it has in its long history been used at times to mean a principle of interpretation, has also had the realist intention, and been used to describe relations which hold outside of the interpreting mind. In the present connection, therefore, this word has both a conceptual or interpretative and an ontological intention.

It will be obvious at a first glance that these categories constitute a very mixed group, but the gathering of them together is not intended to signify that they are all co-ordinate or homogeneous. In fact, their variety reflects the complexity of historical process. Anything simpler, as we shall see, would be an abstract from that process, and, in so far as it claimed to be a complete description of it, fallacious. The category of necessity involves sub-personal, personal and intra-personal elements. That of Providence is predominantly suprapersonal; that of Incarnation is inter-personal (the persons being on the one hand human beings and on the other God); while Freedom and Memory are clearly intra-personal. There is then no attempt made in this classification to obliterate those distinctions that are ultimate for all Christian theology— between God and man, between the Creator and His creatures. Indeed, the danger of this kind of obliteration taking place in this analysis is no greater than it is for any theology of a

Christian nature which asserts that God makes Himself known by sundry mighty acts in history, and that "the Word was made flesh and dwelt among us".

It must further be made clear that we are describing these categories as they are to be found in that unique combination or coalescence of them which takes place in the making of history. There would be many other things that we should want to say about them if, for example, we were writing a complete theology of the Divine Decrees, or of the Doctrine of Grace and Redemption, or an ethical study of moral freedom, or a psychological outline of the nature of human volition. We are looking at these categories from the point of view of history and of how they operate in its construction. A degree of abstraction is involved in that methodological procedure, but it is no greater than that involved in any discussion of one of the great theological doctrines in isolation from the rest.

Next, the question might be raised whether we can legitimately include in any analysis of the categories of history certain events, particularly the Incarnation, which could be rightly said to be "historical". This question is pertinent because we should then be in the position of having to say that while this category (along with the others, of course) is a condition of the possibility of history, it can scarcely be the condition of its own historical actuality. The question is not, however, as unanswerable as it may at first appear, and different replies may be given to it. First, it may be pointed out that the Incarnation is not so much a single event, similar, say, to Caesar's crossing of the Rubicon, as a great complexity of events and of elements, some of which transcend history. It is in virtue of some of these aspects, as will be shown in our later examination of this particular category, that the Incarnation operates as a category, conditioning the nature of all history. This answer would be in line with our recent contention that in speaking of the Incarnation as a category of history we shall not be giving it the kind of treatment that would be demanded in a work on Christology. Secondly, if it is felt that the supra-historical elements in the Incarnation are rooted and grounded in the historical and have no meaning apart from them, then we may make the further reply that it is these supra-historical elements which determine even the historical character of the historical elements. In terms of Cullmann's distinction, it is prophecy that makes history, in those events where the two coincide, and not the reverse, even though the prophecy is rooted in history and is only known and expressed in it. In less ambiguous terms than those which Cullmann uses, it is the transcendent will of God to redeem mankind which is the condition of the empirical events of the Incarnation recorded in the Gospels, and in creating a centre in history God *ipso facto* creates this history, which is to have just this kind of centre.

Against possible objections to what is being done in such a definition of history as that which is here offered, it may be pointed out that this definition does not provide us with a philosophy of history, if it is meant thereby that we have conceived of history as a rationally coherent whole. The fact or the nature of the unitariness of history is not pre-judged in our definition: indeed, the use of the phrase "doctrine" of history is intended to leave the matter open at this stage. The "unitariness" or the "diversity" or "multiformity" of history is one of the problems of history, and it could not therefore be taken as a premise of any analysis of it. Further, it is not claimed that the description of the meaning of history in the terms employed in the definition enables us to see any clear "purpose" running through history, a purpose hidden from the eyes of the technical historian and revealed only to the faithful. Our definition suggests rather that the "meaning" of history is over-simplified if it is reduced to being synonymous with "purpose". The teleological argument, though it has not always gone under this title, has suffered as badly at the hands of historians as it has, in the field of theism, at the hands of philosophers.

CHAPTER THREE

HISTORY AND NECESSITY

I N affirming necessity to be a category within the Christian doctrine of history, it may be thought that we have surrendered our case too early and too unconditionally to three groups of thinkers, the determinists of the Marxist, of the scientific or of the pseudo-Calvinist varieties. By the first group historical activity is construed in terms of economic determinism, so that it becomes the resultant of the economic influences operating at any given moment on the historical agent. Scientific determinism, which has come to exert an authority in a fashion not always consciously recognised in science, which would stoutly reject any reduction of the modes of behaviour which it investigates to purely physical quantities, is prepared to construe historical activity in the crudest mechanistic terms. Pseudo-Calvinism, separating its analysis of the doctrine of Predestination from its proper centre in Christ, and from its paradoxical connection, as stated in Calvin himself, with freedom of the will, is left with an interpretation both of human activity and of history in general which is indistinguishable in anything but name from the determinism of the two previous varieties.

The truth which determinism is endeavouring to state, the truth which becomes the untruth when it is mistaken for the whole account of the matter, is that historical activity does not happen in a vacuum or in an atmosphere of infinite possibility. It happens within a context which has a very fixed rigidity. Both the romanticists and the ethical voluntarists failed to see that human volition occurs within a structure that is in many ways pre-determined, and which the best will in the world cannot ever hope to alter. In fact, the whole discussion of the ethical problem of free-will and determinism was conducted on the false assumption that the truth was to be found only in one or other of these points of view. For this reason, it was easy for either side to show the incompleteness of the views held by the other, and for the discussion to end in stalemate.

20

For this category in its several expressions, and these are more varied than even the determinists realised, sets fixed limits within which the others must operate. For example, human freedom finds itself continually restricted in its range of choices by circumstances beyond its control. Even Providence cannot offer to Solon the range of political possibilities that confronted Stephen Langton. Karl Mannheim (*Man and Society*) in his discussion of the place of freedom in a planned society of the kind forced upon all countries by the very nature of total war, finds such freedom as is now possible at the interstices of the planned economy. It is in some such manner that we are here conceiving of the relation of necessity to the other categories which have been listed, including that of freedom. The naturalistic fallacy in the realm of historical analysis arises when the category of necessity is equated with the system of natural law, when history is reduced to being continuous with Nature and its true character thus denied.

Strange as it may seem, the affirmation of the category of necessity within a Christian doctrine of history is a direct implication of the doctrine of Creation. In one sense the various forms which the category takes constitute the limitations of our creaturely position in the world. We are not "as Gods" who can completely transcend the process either in knowledge or in action. By this we do not imply that the forms of the category of necessity are immediately identifiable with the orders of creation (*Schöpfungsordnungen*) set up by God to ensure the maintenance and continuance of orderliness in a world that might otherwise fall into chaos. They are both wider and more general and narrower than these orders— wider and more general in the sense that they constitute limits by which these orders of creation are themselves bound, and narrower in that they do not include some of these orders which are in fact more directly associable with some of the other categories. But they nevertheless belong to the original structure of creation and form the boundary beyond which no creature can pass. Since the doctrine of Creation is not a true description of man without the doctrine of the Fall, it can be seen that the necessity in this category is not one which is only externally imposed: it is also internally situate in the nature of man, as we shall see later. This category, then, gives truth to the statement that man is a *creature* of history. But it is not the whole truth, just because the affirmation of the category is an implicate of the doctrine of Creation. For in terms of the doctrine, created man, even though fallen, carries with him in this state the self-transcendence which is the ground of the possibility of both evil and good. Man is, therefore, a creator in this history, and the purpose of our description of some of the other categories is to demonstrate the forms which such creativity takes. The denial, by the determinists, of such creativity is a misconstruction primarily not of the nature of history or of human volition but of the doctrine of Creation.

The category of necessity, as has been observed, expresses itself in several forms, and to these we shall now turn our attention.

(a) Time

In including Time as a form of the category of necessity, we are not obliged to make a decision from among the various views of the nature of time which have been offered in the history of the study of this subject, by physicists and phil-osophers—as to whether time is an absolute concept (Newton), a relativist concept (modern physics), an intuition of sense (Kant), an unreality characteristic of the realm of appearance (Hegel and Bradley), or an element in a serial universe (J. W. Dunne). For whatever be the philosophical answer to the question of the *nature* of time, time has certain characteristics in relation to history which would have to be affirmed on almost any view of the nature of time. Since it is time in relation to history that is our concern, we may address ourselves to these characteristics. For example, first the irreversibility of time, which was as clearly recognised by Aristotle as by any of the subsequent critics of the "Greek" view of time*—"Time is

---

* *Note.*—The "Greek" view of time. There are several interesting and not completely reconcilable aspects of Aristotle's view of time, as set forth in *Physics*, IV, xi, ff., which may be mentioned :

    (i) Time is not conceived by him primarily as movement: it is a *scale* by which we estimate movement numerically.

    (ii) Since time is measured by a revolving sphere, or a circle, time comes to be regarded as itself, coming round: "There is a sort of circle of time" (*Physics*, IV, xiv, 23b).

the calculable measure or dimension of motion with respect to *before-and-after-ness*" (*Physics*, IV, xi, 219b, Loeb translation)—imposes the limitation upon the historical agent that once an event has taken place it cannot be undone. We may endeavour to counteract in the present the effects of it; we may repent of its ever having happened, but as an event in the past it cannot be recalled for any reshaping that we later think to be desirable. But the present no less carries its own necessity with it. The fact that a responsibility exists *now*, the fact that an opportunity is now open for me to take a certain line of political or economic action, give to that responsibility and that opportunity a necessity which would be absent from those which are past or future. "Now is the accepted time" is the heightened and intensified Biblical form of the constraint which the present exerts. Inversely, the future, just because it is the not-yet, puts beyond the range of possibility alternative courses of action and by doing so substantially limits historical action with a necessity comparable, though different in basis, to that exerted by the past. To the present the future may seem full of infinite possibilities, but not only are these impossible possibilities for the present, but also the passage of time from present to future will inevitably have reduced the number and range of these possibilities.

Secondly, while it is true, and must be said, that the past is irrevocable from the standpoint of the present, and the present will have become irrevocable when the future has become the present, nevertheless there is a sense in which the past lives on into the present and the present continues into the future, to constitute for both the present and the future the given-ness from which they must make their departure. No

---

(iii) Together with these views he affirms that time is a continuous flux—could it be that O. Cullmann derives his notion of the *continuity* of the time-line ultimately from Aristotle? The *continuity* of the time-line is not a Biblical notion—for time is the countable thing that we are counting.

(iv) The question of interest in relating time to history is: does the Greek cyclical view of history derive from the Greek view of time, or is the derivation the reverse? The answer suggested by the evidence from Aristotle's *Physics* is that the Greek view of time certainly does not derive from the view of history but from the practical situation of measuring time.

historical agent ever commences *de novo*: the "men" are already
on the board when he takes up his responsibilities; he does not
put them there, though he very often wishes that he had, for
the game would be so much easier. The fact that the last player
on the board made certain moves limits definitely the number of
possibilities open to him now; and in the same way his moves
will further limit the person who takes up where he left off.

Thirdly, change is one of the empirical evidences for the
necessity attached to time. Growth and decay, coming-to-be
and passing-away are the necessary characteristics of existents
in time, whether we are thinking of individuals or communities
or societies or whole civilisations. Commenting upon Plato's
view of time, given in the Timaeus, as "the moving image of
eternity", A. E. Taylor draws attention to the close connection
for Plato between Time and the "passage" of Nature when he
says: "Time is not the same thing as γένεσις or τὸ γίγνεσθαι
but a numerical measure of it. . . . Passage is a permanent
character by which Nature is distinguished from that which is
above Nature" (*Commentary on the Timaeus*, p. 689). Nature
is not history, but historical agents are part of Nature, even
if they also transcend Nature, and the extent of this participation in Nature is the guarantee of their coming-to-be and
passing-away. There are no more tragic disillusionments
in the story of mankind than those associated with the discovery of the impermanence of human institutions. The
tragedy lies not in the impermanence of these institutions as
parts of Nature, but in the fact that this impermanence is
heightened because man, who is both a member of Nature
and, as Plato says, "above nature", forgets the former fact;
accordingly, he expects his institutions to have permanent
stability, and fails to detect the decay operative within them,
thus accelerating the process which brings about their disintegration. So basic is this form of the category of necessity
that it has informed the judgment of history held by thinkers
so widely separated in time and outlook as Aristotle, Vico,
Spengler and Toynbee. But in each one of these cases,
naturalism has prevented the exponent from appreciating the
full extent of the influence of this category upon historical
process. History is more than Nature, even if a part of Nature,

and this transcendence introduces into history a dimension
of decay and a speed of disintegration to which there is no
parallel in Nature.

(b) Geography

The necessity exerted by geography need only be stated to
be recognised.   History textbooks abound in evidence for it,
ranging from the Greek city-states to the "arrested civilisation"
of the Eskimos, from the part which the English Channel played
in the events of 1940 to the disastrous rôle of the Burmese
jungle two years later.   On the other hand, there is the fantastic
coinage of the phrase "human geography", which indicates the
recognition by some geographers of the same set of facts, when
looked at from the standpoint of their science.   We might
permissibly include in this same expression of the category
of necessity within the geographical grouping that exerted
by national temperament and outlook.   The latter are, of
course, not wholly due to geography, for past national history
enters in also as influencing national outlook, but it is most
important to recognise the limiting condition which national
loyalties impose even upon men of good will who endeavour
to stand outside of the "party" or "national line".   It is no
longer necessary to emphasise this point as it might have been
twenty years ago in the optimistic days of the League of Nations.
The dreary processes of visas, fingerprinting and passports
tell their own eloquent story.

The affirmation of the necessary quality of the limitations
imposed by national temperament and outlook upon historical
activity has three implications for our modern situation.
First, it leads to a radical scepticism about the possibility of
the establishment of a world state, except under the domination
of one single triumphant power.   Given the constitution of
the political world as we have it today, world peace will be not
the consequence of a universal Utopian conviction of the
brotherhood of man, but the result, almost in a mechanical
sense, of national self-interests organised with cold-blooded
calculation.   There was a good deal more realism—and the
consequences were very much less disastrous—in the seven-
teenth to nineteenth century concept of the balance of power

than in the twentieth century delusions about purity of motives where national self-interest is at stake, and about the "good of mankind" being an object of genuine sacrifice for particular nations.   Secondly, it reveals a fallacy which has supplied terrifying depth to twentieth century history, namely, that world peace has always been but one remove from the *status quo*, and that it was to be reached by the simple—if, also, excessively costly—liquidation of that single obstacle in its achievement.   For that single obstructive nation in each case envisaged ends that were opposed to the self-interest of its neighbours, as well as to the harmony of the world.   So, the fallacy of the once-removed world peace led to the disaster of total war, and further—here the fullest implications of the fallacy emerge—to the disaster of total defeat.   The vacuum created in Europe by the liquidation of Germany is more than any other single thing the source of our present distress.   To change the figure, there is no modern balance of power, because we have destroyed the very nation that might have supplied the fulcrum for such a balance.   Thirdly, the necessary conditioning influence of nationality is also to be detected in less hostile areas than those already mentioned, namely, in the realm of ideas and values.   Truth and freedom have obviously different connotations in East and West.   But even between, say, America and Britain, there are differences of which we are not always conscious when we emphasise our opposition to the Russian point of view.   For example, democracy in a federated union has not only a different method of operation but also a different basis of existence from what it has when combined with limited monarchy.   There may also be differences in the relation of constitutional power to academic freedom, which are only now being brought to light.   An exploration of these differences-in-agreement must be the constant task of two nations which have become so closely linked in policy, sympathy and destiny.

(c) Socio-economic Origin and Status

The necessity which operates through socio-economic origin and status is not here affirmed in the crude senses, either of complete Marxism, which would exclude any of the other categories involved in historical process, or of that which regards all other forms of human behaviour and activity as functions (in the mathematical rather than the physiological sense) of the socio-economic. There are too many instances of what I should call partial transcendence of socio-economic origin in the human narrative for the former to be any more than a doctrinaire thesis; while the various branches of human thought and action exhibit too great a degree of autonomy for the latter to deserve either a *prima facie* or an ultimate credence. Granted such partial transcendence and such autonomy, the truth remains that no matter how far a human historical agent travels from his socio-economic origins and endeavours to change his status, he carries with him the traces of the rock from whence he was hewn. These traces take the form of prejudices, ways of looking at things, a certain sense of values, even the memory of what he once was, which cannot be finally eradicated. Even when he reacts most violently against them, his reaction itself is determined by that which produces it. In fact, in some ways, polar reaction exerts greater deter-mining influence on historical behaviour than those traces which persist in the positive form.

Socio-economic status would seem to exert an almost determining influence upon the historical agent in at least two respects. First, the intellectual judgment of a political or social or economic situation upon which any action must be based is necessarily a perspectival judgment: it is a view taken from a point within one specific group, and it will bear all the evidence of sharing the presuppositions of that group, as has just been seen in relation to the effects of socio-economic origins. We are not for the present raising the question of whether a perspectival judgment can ever achieve truth or whether historic judgment must always remain relativist and therefore untrue. But it is contended that it is impossible for anyone to make a historical judgment from a point beyond this or that perspective, and that scientific objectivity in history is not to be achieved within historical criticism by illusions of this sort. The way to objectivity, if the term is to be retained, is by the most careful comparison of several perspectival judgments, a comparison which will involve the bringing to light, as far as possible, of the presuppositions implicit in the different perspectives.

To stop our account here would, however, commit us to an over-intellectualised account of the influence of socio-economic status upon historical judgment and action. For there is a second and no less important way in which this influence operates, namely in this, that the historical agent is *emotionally* conditioned by his status. The Trade Union member has acquired a certain pattern of emotional reaction to the problems of industry and commerce, as have the owner, and the member of the public who is not a Trade Union member. Equally, the minister of a Church has a pattern of emotional reaction to the members of his congregation, to ministers of other denominations, and to the great issues with which the Church is faced in our time. Again, it is a perspectival reaction, but it is one which is more difficult to transcend, because it issues from profounder depths of the personality than does the intellectual reaction. This emotional pattern sets very definite limits both to human sympathy and love towards, and consequently to human understanding of, those who do not share the perspective. A reasonable-minded owner may think that he understands and appreciates the reasons for a strike, but he can never feel these reasons in his bones in the way in which the union member can and does; so long as he does not feel these reasons "where it hurts", even his intellectual understanding and appreciation fall short. Also, while it may be possible by comparison of perspectival judgments to arrive at something which approximates even more closely to a trans-subjective judgment, it is impossible to compound emotional reactions into any comparable unity. There is no higher synthesis which will accommodate the thesis and antithesis of love and hatred or of self-interests on both sides. Forgiveness, reconciliation, is the only hope, but it negates, and does not synthesise both the thesis and the antithesis.

What, in effect, is here being argued is that atomic individualism is quite inadequate to the description or explanation of the complexities of historical process. Historical man is man-in-community; his understanding of a social or economic situation is in large part a group-understanding, and his reaction to a political crisis is, to a great extent, a group-reaction. As his economic activities are woven into the complex tissue of modern industrialism or commercialism, so his emotional reactions are woven into a tissue with those of his social confreres. For this reason, historiography in the "heroes and hero-worship" tradition must ever remain an artificial abstraction, for the "hero" is always more a product of his age and group than the "worshipper" can properly appreciate. In fact, if the truth were told, the "heroics" of the "hero" have very often consisted in a certain dexterity in exploiting his oneness with the group mind and emotions. However, in terms of our general principle concerning the relation of the category of necessity to the others, it must be emphasised that socio-economic status, while it functions as a limiting condition for the historical agent, is not a completely determining condition; and to that extent part of the truth must be recognised as lying with the Kingsley tradition.

(d) Human Self-interest

It might appear desirable to some that we designate this form of the category of necessity "sin" at the outset. I have declined to do so not only because the term "sin" at once introduces the theological question and involves also the notion of free defiance of God, but also because its existence is attested by writers who do not hold Christian presuppositions or who, if they do, feel no obligation to employ them in the description of this phenomenon. This bias to self-interest is observed in the psychological hedonism which is a most curious and in some ways stultifying concomitant to Kant's rationalistic ethics, and which, despite all their obvious differences, brings him very close to the English and Scottish Sentimentalists. It was the honest recognition of this fact in human nature which shattered the tidy coherence of J. S. Mill's universal Utilitarianism. The Marxists use it to incite the proletariat against the bourgeousie and the capitalists, naïvely unaware that it is as likely to disrupt any proletariat community as it is to disrupt the present "evil age". The depth psychologists are acutely aware of its existence, but they seem to forget, if indeed they ever knew, that it is just as comfortably at home in the Super-ego as it is in the abominable Id, and that no amount of psychiatric alchemy can transform self-interest into altruism. But whereas the theorists, ethical, economic, and psychological, have failed to embody this fundamental aspect of human behaviour in a rationally coherent system, ordinary human society in its wisdom has accepted it as the basis of all systems of justice. These systems represent a balance struck between the interests of my neighbour and myself, which we can only with hypocrisy ultimately deny, and between those of both of us and those of the society as a whole of which we are parts. So much of what we regard as commendable self-restraint and self-denial is, as Professor Butterfield points out (*Christianity and History*, p. 30), only the restraint imposed upon us by a society which knows all too well what stuff we are made of, and regards such restraint to be one of the price conditions of its survival. For this reason he speaks of cupidity and self-interest as supplying "a gravitational pull in history" (id., p. 41).

But the presence of the "gravitational pull" and the influence which it exerts in history are often not readily detectable because of the way in which it endeavours to be other than what it really is. The self-righteousness which accompanies self-interest gives to the latter a deeper dimension of seriousness and lends to it still greater determining influence than it would otherwise have. If it operated *simpliciter*, we could read off from history those events which were patently motivated by it, and separate on the other side those events which had nobler sources. But just because it occurs all too rarely in the unmixed form, its presence is to be suspected everywhere, and not least of all in those persons and institutions which most explicitly disavow it. Because of its subtlety, it cannot be detected always by the agents themselves in history, or even if detected, it is very swiftly rationalised, and consequently exerts an almost demonic determinism in human activity. To make things more difficult, it is more readily observable in others than in ourselves. Accordingly, the systems of justice which endeavour to maintain the balance between conflicting interests within communities are never absolutely just. They reflect in greater or less degree the triumph of the interests of the powerful

group in politics or the economic field, which because of its
fear for its position is slightly and sometimes exceedingly more
insistent on its own rights than need be. Therein perhaps
lies the simplest refutation of the theory of the "contractual"
basis of society: no group, except the dominant group, would
ever endorse the inequalities and injustices that form the
fabric of most historic societies.

(e) Inner Dynamism

I have found it almost impossible to select any single word
or phrase to cover this final expression of the category of
necessity, and must instantly hasten to explain what I mean by
"inner dynamism". It is the case in history that the results
that issue from the individual decisions of persons and from the
collective decisions of groups exceed immeasurably both the
intentions and the expectations entertained by the persons or
groups at the time of making the decisions. Butterfield conceives of this result in terms of a compounding of wills or at
least of their effects (op. cit., p. 93). But his own illustrations
which immediately follow suggest that this description is not
quite complete. The production of the capitalist system was,
as he points out, the decision of no one person; but neither
was it the decision of any group-will, nor simply the compounding of wills within the community. Butterfield brings
his account of the situation into line when he speaks of this
"kind of history-making which goes on so to speak over our
heads" (op. cit., p. 94). This addition to what was intended
either by the individual or the group, this extra which works
itself out with an uncontrollable necessity, uncontrollable
because it is unobserved at the time of its occurrence, is what I
intend by the inner dynamism of history.

The writers on history who have drawn attention to this
aspect of it have, on the whole, tended to identify it with
Providence. For example, Butterfield seems to regard it as
a secular type of Providence, and at times almost equates it
with Divine Providence. Bossuet writes: "[All who govern]
do more or less than they intend, and their counsels have never
failed to have unforeseen effects" (Discours, E.T., p. 405,
quoted by Löwith, Meaning in History, p. 142). Vico, who

writes: "The civil world issued from a mind contrary and always superior to the particular ends that men have proposed to themselves", did not hesitate to identify this form of the category of necessity with Divine Providence, though it is doubtful whether in his hands the idea of Providence differs greatly from that secular type which we find in Butterfield. Croce calls it the human "comedy of errors", Hegel "the cunning of reason" in terms of his own philosophy of history, while Ranke thought of an occult force working in the midst of apparent confusion, though even in him the notion has the theological connection—see his letter of 1820: ". . . Especially do we find it (God's name) in the connecting line that runs through History" (quoted in P. Geyl, *From Ranke to Toynbee*, p. 7).

For my own part, I find it undesirable to identify the inner dynamism within history with Providence, for several reasons: To begin with, the decree of Providence has in the history of Christian theology been associated with at least three things —with God's bringing good out of evil, with God's bringing judgment upon evil, and with God's working out of some over-all purpose in history. Now it appears to me that no one of these three things can be regarded as a characteristic feature of what has here been termed inner dynamism. In the situation to which our phrase refers, on occasions an apparently inordinate amount of evil has been brought into existence out of what, if it were not completely good, was certainly not as evil as the consequences would lead us to believe. In these situations, too, because of this disproportion, even the eye of faith cannot detect any reason why the evil thus consequent should be regarded as judgment, should be regarded as the judgment of God on previous evil, except in the most general terms in which one might say that all evil is God's judgment on previous evil—though such terms would be so general as to make everything that happens a judgment upon everything that has gone before. Nor can this inner dynamism be equated with a purpose which comprehends the whole of history: it is rather a category which operates at different historical periods which are isolable from each other. That is, it makes no attempt to link up those isolable periods with one another, so that in some sense "the meaning" of one period can be shown to carry over into the next. In fact, there may be periods in history at which it is not obviously operative at all. Now these three features of Providence do not exhaust all that Christian theology has to say on the subject, but it would be agreed that they are necessary to Providence and that whatever did not have them could not be equated with Providence. It is therefore because this inner dynamism does not exhibit these three "marks" of Providence that I would reject any identification of the two.

A second reason for rejecting their identification is the moral ambiguity which attaches to the operation of inner dynamism. On the one hand, it can be construed in an ethically neutral way, when we draw attention simply to the fact that in historical process, from time to time, the effects which follow certain actions of the agents in history exhibit a complexity and range out of all proportion to their intentions. In this case, we are emphasising the fact that, in the situations interpreted by this form of the category of necessity, there is an inexplicable disproportion between the effects historically produced by the volitions of agents and those which they planned, without saying whether this disproportion is a good or a bad thing. On the other hand, we may construe this form of the category of necessity in a manner which does justice to the *mixed* moral quality both of the causes and of the effects, both of the agents' volitions and of the results that follow from them in the course of history. That is, we are not saying simply that good came out of evil, or evil out of good, or even that evil was followed by worse evil because of God's judgment upon it, but rather that, from a situation which contained a mixture of good and evil, another situation followed which had a more complexly interwoven tissue of good *and* evil, and that no point-to-point causal correlation can be established between this new situation and that which preceded it. It is this moral ambiguity attaching to the inner dynamism, as I have called it, which makes it something less than Providence. This conclusion would be in line with the fact that inner dynamism is empirically observable by technical historians who have no theological presuppositions in their analysis and description of history, and who, in their so-called "scientific" approach, have explicitly rejected the notion of a Prime Cause, and confined themselves to secondary causes.

To say so much is not, however, to deny that inner dynamism is related to Providence. It is so related, but not in a more specific way than are any of the other forms of the category of necessity. It constitutes a limit within which Providence must work, if, like the other forms, too, it may be a medium through which God providentially works; for God may turn both the wrath of men and the compound evil effects of their actions to His glory. At present, our interest is in inner dynamism as a form of the category of necessity. As such, it emphasises the fact to which we have already drawn attention, namely, that man is a creature of history, as well as the creator of it.

One clear implication of this inner dynamism is that man is, as Professor Niebuhr describes him, a "creature of history". Accumulated history, with its compounding of the results of all previous decisions and events, constitutes a necessary structure which the historical agent at any given moment in history has to accept as unalterable in many respects. But, further, it has to be emphasised that he himself is part of this structure. He is involved in it in an inexorable fashion, limited not only in an objective way by the reduced number of possible lines of action that remain open to him, but also in a subjective way by the reduced number of possible emotional, volitional and cognitional reactions which he is capable of making to any given situation. The category of necessity, therefore, cannot be stated solely in extra-personal terms so that the "internal life" of man in history remains a field of undetermined and unlimited choice. Its full implications penetrate to the very heart of human historical activity, as it operates from within as well as from without.

CHAPTER FOUR

HISTORY AND PROVIDENCE

PROVIDENCE is that decree whereby God wills in eternity that which comes to pass in time. Such a description is by its very nature formal, and the full significance of Providence can be understood only when we pay attention to the second part of it, the working out of the decree in time, which yields us its content. In a way, Providence is implied by Creation. Such is the God who creates that He cannot be Himself and have no concern for, or take no active interest in, the beings whom He has created to find their fullest peace and fulfilment in dependence upon him and in worship of Him. Deism, then, is a contradiction not only of the doctrine of Providence but also of that of Creation. In Providence the Creator-God relates Himself to His creatures and actually becomes involved in the created order. Now God's Providence obviously takes many forms, all of which are not immediately relevant to our purpose. For example, God's Providence is the source of all the "mercies that are new every morning": food and drink, love and friendship, health and strength, and so on. While it is true that human historical agents in every age and country have had their share of all those benefits, and while there would be no history as we know it without them, for our present purpose we must limit our description of the category of Providence to those aspects of it which are particularly significant for history.

Accordingly we shall deal first of all with Divine Sovereignty, by which notion we intend that God is the Lord not only of the stars in their courses, but of human affairs in all their intricacy and complexity. It is because He is Lord that God providentially regards and governs the whole of Creation. An awareness of this fact marks the great step from a particularist religion to one that is universalist, an awareness which was one of the greatest gifts of the Hebrew mind to the understanding of history, an awareness which in its profoundest moments it recognised to be a gift of God to the nation. In fact, the true statement of the situation is that Israel came to an understanding of Creation from their awareness of God's Sovereignty in history. No other view is possible if we take seriously God's historical Revelation of Himself, and the fact that Israel's is a historical religion. The nature of Divine Providence is understood only when it is related to the Christian doctrine of salvation. Karl Barth's contention (*The Doctrine of the Word of God*, 1/1, E.T., p. 351) that "God is the Lord" is the content of the Christian Revelation has been the subject of recent discussion (C. Welch, *The Trinity in Contemporary Theology*, pp. 168 ff., and L. Hodgson, *The Journal of Theological Studies*, N.S., vol. I, pp. 52 f.), but it is true in this regard that the Sovereignty of God, His Lordship, is integrally involved in and revealed through the Revelation in Jesus Christ, both in His Person and in His Work. What might be called the pattern of the redemption wrought in Jesus Christ—the judgment of God upon all sin, the mercy of God in forgiveness of sin and God's purpose not to allow the judgment to be brought to nought or the forgiveness to be scorned in the historical lives of human beings—is the expression of the true nature of God's Sovereignty, and the archetype of God's providential working throughout history. It is not only that we are first sure of salvation in Jesus Christ, and that we argue inductively to the Lordship of God and to His providential guiding of the Universe as the grounds both of the actuality and of the possibility *for us* of this salvation, but that the manner in which God works and reveals Himself in Jesus Christ *is* the manner in which He works providentially throughout the whole of history. On these terms, too, the "Cosmic Christ" type of Christology is an essential moment in all true Christian thinking concerning Christ, and not an arbitrary development of it in one specific cultural milieu. So God's providential working under the Old Covenant, and under His uncovenanted mercies, is prophetic of the mighty work which He did in Christ; and under the New Covenant, it becomes the fulfilment of what was begun in that mighty work. When, therefore, we relate Divine Providence to the Redemptive Work of God in Jesus Christ, and *ipso facto* to the Sovereignty of God, the discernible pattern of Providence is seen to be—judgment, mercy and redemptive purpose.

To go so far is to have anticipated what will be said concerning Incarnation, but so much must be said at this stage for two reasons. On the one hand, there is the continual danger in Christian theology of isolating doctrine from doctrine, and of failing to explore the profound effects which the Incarnation produces upon our understanding of all our other doctrines. In the present reference, this danger would take the form of suggesting that God acts in one way in redemption and in another in Providence. Surely, among other things the Incarnation integrates our appreciation of *how* God works. On the other hand, Providence is a category in its own right within the Christian doctrine of history. While it is related to Incarnation and only properly understood when so related, Providence operates across the whole of history, whereas Incarnation occurs at a definite and limited period. It assists both in making history what it is for the Christian and, within the limits of the Divine economy of salvation, in preparing the way for the central events in that economy.

Providence, then, exhibits the characteristics of judgment, mercy and redemptive purpose. God's judgment is seen in the manner in which disaster finally overtakes those who deny the Sovereignty of God and arrogate to themselves the attributes of self-sufficiency, independence, complete moral virtue and lordship which are the proper attributes only of God Himself. As St. Anselm would say, the moral order and beauty of the universe cannot be violated without God demonstrating the consequences which flow therefrom. God's mercy, on the other hand, is seen in the fact that God so often gives time for repentance. The Nemesis is not always as swift as the moral depravity merits. Perhaps the book of Jonah is the best expression, within the Old Testament at least, of this aspect of Divine mercy. His mercy is seen in the manner in which He touches the hearts of men and nations and brings them to that repentance which is the human ground of forgiveness.

One of its clearest expressions in the New Testament is in Romans, 8.26: "And we know that all things work together for good to them that love God, to them who are the called according to this purpose"; while the redemptive purpose in Providence is stated at Romans, 8.32: "He that spared not His own Son, but delivered Him up for us all, how shall He not with Him also freely give us all things?" This passage is particularly interesting for our purpose in the manner in which it links Providence with Incarnation, and makes the latter the ground for, and the guarantee of, the former. In virtue of the Incarnation, Providence is harnessed to the mercy and the love of God; without the Incarnation the relation between the two remains ambiguous.

It must now be clear that the view that history is the story of fallen man's sustained and unbroken defiance of God can be no part of the Christian doctrine of history. For such a view involves a denial of the many occasions on which the Divine providential mercy has turned the stony hearts of men to hearts of flesh and love, and a virtual exclusion of God from the world which He has created.

To elucidate further this category of Providence, we make the following comments:

(a) This category operates within the limiting terms of the categories of necessity and freedom. There are some facts in the necessary structure of history which even Providence cannot change, and which we cannot expect it to change when we ourselves are called upon to act in a specific historical situation, a point always to be remembered in our prayers. On the other hand, and, as it were, at the other extreme, the Divine initiative of mercy does not destroy or hold no respect for the freedom of the agents in the historical process. Repentance is not forced upon individuals in the way in which judgment apparently is. Butterfield describes the situation in the following terms: "There is no symbolic representation that will do justice to history save (that of the composer) who composes the music as we go along, and, when we slip into aberrations, switches his course in order to make the best of everything" (*Christianity and History*, p. 109). While Butterfield has, by this illustration from music, done justice to the category of freedom, it would appear that he has done so at the expense of misrepresenting some of the essential features of Providence. For example, the question might be asked whether Providence has not an overruling purpose beyond the purposes of the individual persons and groups which act in history. In other words, the rôle of Providence in history is certainly partially posterior to specific events in history ("God turns even the wrath of men to His praise"), but in order to be so it must be also prior to and contemporaneous with these events. Besides, the illustration suffers from the defect of all aesthetic interpretations of the world and history, namely, of failing to do justice to the irrationalities and the evils which can be built into no conceivable harmony. In saying so we do not simply mean that some things which are unharmonious to us could possibly be embodied in a higher harmony by a master-composer: rather, there are certain disharmonies which, even on our limited standards, we judge must be still more cacophonous to someone with a more delicate ear and with higher standards of appreciation. In other words, there are evils which cannot be transvalued by God, things which offend us but which must offend Him infinitely more, because of His absolute moral goodness and profound perspicacity, and irrationalities which even the Divine Wisdom could not rationalise without denying His very nature.

(b) In assigning to Providence a prior and contemporaneous as well as a posterior rôle in history we have stumbled upon one of the most difficult problems in all Christian dogmatics— the relation of Providence to human freedom. How can God's providential ordering of history be reconciled with any honest postulation of human freedom in historical activity? It is substantially the same problem which in the field of Christian ethics we call the problem of grace and freedom. The usual and only answer is to admit in humility that we are here in the presence of one of the profoundest paradoxes in the Christian faith. The existence of this paradox raises the problem of the relations of the categories, which we have enunciated, to one another ; and it is one which shall be dealt with later in the terms of the concept of dimensions and structures within history. But for the present we may say that the fundamental and indissoluble nature of the paradox is to be seen in the facts that either arm of the paradox taken by itself fails patently to convey the truth about the situation, and that when we find ourselves "existentially" involved in historical activity, and when we reflect upon our own past, we find that there is no inherent incompatibility in the two affirmations, that is, of Providence and freedom. It is relevant, too, that those who deny freedom in favour of some kind of providential determinism, for example, the Marxists, nevertheless use the language which implies moral responsibility, and therefore moral freedom. On the contrary, those who deny Providence in favour of freedom find themselves inclining to a type of secular Providence such as that held by some technical historians. A paradox is therefore preferable to any penultimate resolutions which oversimplify the situation described by the paradox, or tacitly reintroduce it.

(c) The category of Providence is the basis of the unitariness of history (cf. R. Niebuhr, *Faith and History*, p. 127). It is essential at once to clarify all that is intended by this proposition. Clearly it is not meant that history is an empirically observable whole, a whole which can be discerned by the unbeliever and the believer alike; or that it is an empirical unity for the believer with all the insights of his faith. The unitariness of history is an implication of the singleness of the will of God who is Sovereign in history. Once we allow that the historical order is part of God's creation, once we say, as we must on the basis of our knowledge of God derived from Hebrew-Christian history, that this God providentially orders the course of history so that His purpose for man and Creation shall not finally be frustrated, then dualism or pluralism in the analysis of history becomes ultimately unthinkable.

(d) But the fragmentariness of history has to be affirmed as well as its unitariness, and on the same basis, that of Divine Providence. For a providential God history will have unity, but for anyone less than God the fragmentariness is all that is observable. This view can be affirmed without resorting to language about God being above history or beyond it, and without committing ourselves to the statement that God is "in" history. That is, while we may affirm the form of Providence, we cannot always specify the content which that form will take at any given time in the historical process. Such fragmentariness will prevent us from premature

conjectures of the "lo here, lo there" variety, which endeavour
to see the "hand of God" where it need not necessarily be. A
serious conviction about the fragmentariness of history would
deter me, therefore, from establishing too close a nexus
between the "inconclusiveness of history" and the Last Judgment (R. Niebuhr, op. cit., p. 143). For while admittedly
some of the "inconclusiveness of history" is due to what is
called its moral obscurity, that is, to what seems an ill-pro-
portioned distribution of deserts for moral virtue and vice,
still some of the inconclusiveness must be a consequence of
our creaturely status within the historical order. In other
words, the fragmentariness of history is due on the human side
both to man's creatureliness and to his sin, and not to either by
itself. Besides, the Last Judgment is implied not so much by
the "inconclusiveness of history" as by the very nature of
Christ's first coming, for it constitutes the consummation of
the work which He initially did while upon earth. To separate
it from the latter and to link it with the inconclusiveness of
history is to lay it open to the danger of being regarded as a
type of wish-fulfilment, a pious hope that right will be done
in the end.

(e) But the fragmentariness of history would also appear to
be within the Divine economy of salvation. For it just is the
case—man's sin and creatureliness are not in themselves
sufficient explanation—that God has elected to reveal Himself
at some points of history more than at others, or, more exactly,
rather than at others. We do not describe the situation
adequately if we simply say that God is revealing Himself all
the time and that sinful men cannot detect His working in the
events in which they are involved. In fact, there is no Biblical
evidence whatsoever for the view that God is revealing His
providential purpose all the time, and that we cannot observe
it for one reason or another. The argument that He is is a very
bad *argumentum a silentio*. God's Providence seems to be
more closely related to some events in history than to others,
and this association belongs to the Divine intention and is not
merely an accommodation to human fallibility or sin. The
Deus Revelatus is also the *Deus Absconditus*, and while of late
we are coming to say that He is *absconditus* at the very moment

D

of being *revelatus*, we cannot afford to forget the other truth that He is often *absconditus* when He is quite definitely not *revelatus*. "Am I not a God afar off as well as a God that is nigh?" (Jeremiah, 23.23). The history of Israel is to be understood only in terms of the increasing complexity and profundity of this association of God with specific events, but throughout this association it retains its *mise-en-scène* in the actuality of historical occurrence.

(*f*) It might seem that we have involved ourselves in the contradiction of affirming both the unitariness and the fragmentariness of history, but the examination of this possible contradiction will assist us in understanding further what is meant by these two terms. The contradiction might be avoided if we said that history is unitary for God and fragmentary for us, except in so far as God, through His Revelation of Himself and of His purposes, makes known to us in some measure its unitariness. I should prefer to say, however, that for God, while history is unitary, since it is the domain of His Sovereignty, it is not unified. As we have already seen in discussing Butterfield's illustration of the composer and the orchestra, there are certain things within history, irrationalities and evils, which cannot be included in some comprehensive system in which they lose their essential character. They persist even in a universe where God is Sovereign, and they will persist until the Last Judgment. It is the existence of these which makes history so fragmentary for us—but this fragmentariness is not an illusion belonging to the "Appearance" in which it is our lot to live, and disappearing in the "Absolute"; it is as real to God as it is to us. We do not yet see "all things put under Him", but their destiny is that they shall be; and when they are, this fragmentariness will have disappeared.

(*g*) It is the reality of this fragmentariness of history which would lead me to question the continuity of the "redemption-line" which Cullmann traces through history. Since the Bible would appear to know nothing of the continuity of which Cullmann speaks it would be interesting to learn whence he derived the notion. It would be, to say the least, embarrassing, if, after all, the origin of this idea of continuity were Greek.

We have not only Aristotle's explicit statement that "time is a
continuous flux" (*Physics*, IV, xi, 219b) but also the whole
interest of the pre-Socratics in the nature of infinity, which is
the same problem as that of continuous series. It may be,
simply, that Cullmann has unwittingly accepted an evolutionary
type of theory concerning the nature of history and transcribed
it into his own terms of the redemptive time-line. This
suggestion would be confirmed by his otherwise un-Biblical
and incomprehensible statement that the redemptive time-line
is *upward sloping*. But the Hebrew mind and the Christian mind
(even when it is Hellenistically inclined) within the limits
of Old and New Testament thought have shown no concern
about the problems of philosophy and physics connected with
infinity and continuity; whereas the introduction of evolutionary concepts into the interpretation of the Biblical view of
time and history is the grossest anachronism and immediately
invalidates any theory which commits this sort of error.

(*h*) So far I have not explicitly used the term "grace".
It has been implied, of course, in the very notion of Providence,
and also in that of Mercy. Of all human history, it is true that
"it is of God's mercy that we are not consumed", so that in a
certain sense even God's judgments in history are less severe
than absolute and solitary justice would demand that they
should be. But it is valuable to discriminate four ways in which
God's grace is involved in history, three of which answer
fairly accurately to what some call three modes of revelation.

(1) There is that general Providence which we have already
noted, according to which God provides for the needs of all
men. This idea could also be described by the orthodox
notion of "common grace".

(2) There is that more special gracious activity of God in
relation to the people of Israel, which while it is particularist
in its setting is nevertheless universal in its implications.

(3) There is the once-for-all action of Divine grace in the
events of the Incarnation, when "the Word dwelt among us
full of grace and truth".

(4) Such a description of the situation would be incomplete
without our taking into account God's gracious actions in the
hearts of men whereby they become aware in penitence and

humility of each of these other three expressions of Divine Providence. This work of God is normally associated with the Holy Spirit in Christian doctrine: as Barth says, God from beneath meets God from above. This gracious indwelling of God through His Spirit is obviously of the greatest importance in any analysis of the Christian categories of history, for the actions of Spirit-possessed men have often determined the course of the historical process.

When, therefore, we turn to the category of Incarnation, we remain within the realm of grace, but we are studying a unique expression of it, so unique that it amounts to another category of it, one which, in fact, as we have already seen, is regulative of that of Providence.

CHAPTER FIVE

HISTORY AND THE INCARNATION

(a) THE INCARNATION AS FULFILMENT

O BVIOUSLY it is not our purpose here to give anything like a complete Christology, nor need we think it necessary to do so. A complete Christology would be interested in the wider questions of Revelation and the relation of Jesus Christ to God, in the issue of the One Person and the two Natures which is still, whatever else we say, the ultimate problem of Christology; but we draw a narrower compass, and investigate the place which the Incarnation occupies within the historical process. The wider Christological insights will be drawn upon, but it must not be thought that we are here committed to defining them all. It is necessary to state this methodological delimitation, for otherwise our account of the Incarnation will appear inadequate, or we may seem to be too interested in the human, historical side of this central doctrine of the Christian faith and too little concerned with the more important matter of the relation of the Incarnation to the mind, will and nature of God.

By the Incarnation I intend those events which form the subject of the Four Gospels, of which we make profession in the second paragraph of the Apostles' Creed, and which have been variously described as "God's becoming man", "God's entering history", "God's becoming one with us that we might become one, or at one with Him", and so on. But while by those who use many of these phrases it is usually understood that the Incarnation is something that happens "in" history, the secular course of events providing a framework for the sacred, which can be separated from its earthly structure without any serious loss of content, and in fact with a greatly enhanced possibility of its being understood, we are here maintaining, in accord with our original definition of the "categories of history", that the Incarnation is to be considered along with the other categories, and more importantly than them all, as actually constitutive of history. Presently, then, we are going to discuss the question, not of whether the Incarnation is to be regarded as a literal historical fact, or as a supra-historical event, or whether it stands at the edge of history, but rather of how it is that the Incarnation *makes* history what the Christian believes history to be. The constitutive function of the Incarnation in relation to history may be described in the following way.

One of the commonest contemporary statements concerning Jesus Christ is that He is "the fulfilment of the whole of history", and in this form the claim demands that we examine the place of the concept of fulfilment in our analysis of the categories of a Christian doctrine of history. Two things must be noted, however, at the outset concerning this statement. First of all, the New Testament writers and Jesus Christ Himself did not conceive of the Incarnation primarily in terms of the fulfilment of the whole of history: rather did their interest lie in the fact that it fulfilled all that God had promised in the Old Testament. Had the question been put to them as to whether Christ fulfilled the whole of history, they would no doubt have replied that He did, though "history" in our sense of the term would probably have been a somewhat unfamiliar notion to them. The New Testament thinks of Christ as the One in whom God has accomplished in full all that He had promised to His people throughout their long history, in fact, from the time that He first called Abraham. What exactly the New Testament meant when it described Christ as "fulfilment" is the problem to which our attention must turn, for its meaning is not as clear as is often assumed; nor is the "range" of the fulfilment always precisely defined. The second matter to be noted, therefore, concerning the statement that Jesus Christ is the fulfilment of all history, is that it is a derivative and secondary affirmation, and not primary. It is a deduction from the fact that Jesus Christ fulfils God's promises in the Old Testament; and its truth is to be demonstrated only in that relationship. That is, we cannot expect to validate it by what is called "the appeal to history", as if it were an empirically demonstrable centre from which all historical movements radiated outwards. To

interpret the statement in this derivative and dependent sense
is to put it in its proper context; and, further, to provide for
it the only possible validation that it can have in any Christian
doctrine of history.

When we turn, then, to the claims that Christ primarily
fulfilled all that God had promised and had done under the
Old Testament, we may take as our starting-point the statement that this claim was original to the mind of Jesus Christ.
This statement, no doubt, flies in the face of the whole agnosticism of the Form Critics concerning what was in the mind of
Our Lord, but, in my judgment, this is the point at which we
must decide between Revelation *in* Jesus Christ and Revelation
in the mind of the Primitive Church (i.e., Revelation *concerning* Jesus Christ). Beyond question, fulfilment was an
Ur-word of the Primitive Church, if not in fact *the Ur*-word,
for the description of how to understand the "mission and
message" of Jesus Christ. But it was an *Ur*-word in the
Primitive Church because that was how Jesus first regarded
Himself. It is, of course, arguable that Jesus was the
fulfilment of the Old Testament and that He was not
aware of being so. But the problem at once presents itself of
defining the sense in which He is the Revelation of God. For if
it is the Primitive Church which is the first to apprehend Jesus
Christ as fulfilment, and if such a conception is projected
back into the mind of Jesus Christ by the New Testament
writers, then the conclusion follows that Revelation is something
that happens in the Primitive Church and in the writers of the
New Testament, but not in Jesus Christ. Further, the Revelation of which we are now speaking becomes a Revelation
concerning Jesus Christ and is not Revelation *in* Jesus Christ.
It seems to me to be an incontrovertible first principle both of
our Christology and of our doctrine of Revelation that Jesus
Christ Himself should be aware of that Revelation of which
He is Himself the bearer; and that the understanding both of
who He was and of the Revelation which He bore should have
its roots in His mind. If the Spirit reveals the hidden things
of Christ, it is no less true that it is Christ who has sent Him,
and that the things which the Spirit reveals are not hidden
from Christ as they are from those to whom they are revealed.

Otherwise, the Holy Spirit becomes a kind of *deus ex machina* who injects into the minds of New Testament writers propositions concerning what was happening when "the Word was made flesh", which were not indigenous to the Incarnation itself, and which were not known to the Word at the time of the Incarnation. In effect, the controversy between the Form Critics and some, at least, of their opponents, does not concern only textual or critical matters: it opens up the much vaster question of the nature, content and locus of Revelation. That is, the *kerugma* grew out of what Christ thought and taught concerning Himself; and it was from the contact of their minds with His that the disciples, and through them, the Gospel writers, formulated the message. The events which took place at Emmaus exhibit the pattern which I am seeking to establish: Christ "expounded unto them in all the scriptures the things concerning Himself" (Luke, 24.27). This pattern extended itself into the Primitive Church so that the understanding of Revelation was in fact the understanding of what Christ had said concerning Himself, and not of some addenda extraneous to what He had said.

There has been a great deal of discussion concerning what may be called "the content of Revelation", ranging from the modernist views that it is a way of life, or an ethical example, to Karl Barth's controversial proposition that "God reveals Himself as the Lord". But there is little doubt that the original New Testament conception of the content of the Revelation (though again this is not the language that would have been used) is that Jesus Christ is *fulfilment*. This fact is integral to any contention such as that made by Professor W. Manson (*Jesus the Messiah*, p. 11) that "somewhere, somehow, Jesus before His death stood self-revealed to His disciples as the Messiah". For the Messiah was the Promised One, and it was just because He stood in the organic relation of fulfilment to all that Israel had hoped for on the basis of God's promises that Jesus claimed the title. On these grounds, any evidence which is adduced for the primacy in the consciousness of Jesus of His Messiahship is *ipso facto* evidence for the primacy for Him of His awareness of the fulfilment in Him of all God's promises to Israel.

It has now become customary to refer to the description of Christ as "fulfilment" as the "argument from prophecy". But I doubt whether this type of peripheral allocation does justification to the centrality and the originality of the description both in the history of Christian understanding of Christ and in Christian devotion. The phrase, "the argument from prophecy", carries with it the implications that this "argument" is to be ranked with some other arguments that we might adduce for the Person of Christ or for His claims upon us, and that we need not necessarily accept it if some of the others prove to be more suited to our culture or to "our modern way of looking at things". There is the further implication that even at the beginning men may have come to understand who Christ was by some other means than this "argument", and that they sometimes did and sometimes did not employ it to bolster up a view which really rested on quite different grounds. Therein, to my mind, lies the danger of the use of the term "argument" for the idea of fulfilment, and it was a danger which appeared as soon as the Church relegated the notion of "fulfilment" to the field of apologetics, whereas its rightful place was—and is—within the *kerugma*, and the dogmatic science which endeavours to expound the *kerugma*. For that reason, if we wish to continue to speak of the *argument* from prophecy, then we must also say that it is a *part* of the *kerugma* and not an argument by which we wish to prove its truth, as if the *kerugma* could even be stated without taking it into consideration.

This idea of fulfilment belonged, we might therefore say, to the very given-ness of the situation in which Christ was first known by men for what He really was. Further, it is the ultimate basis upon which rest all the other Christological affirmations that we make. For example, when men saw that He fulfilled so gloriously, and so finally, all that God had promised by His prophets of old, they found that they could do no other than confess "My Lord and my God". Here was the Word spoken by the prophets, fulfilled beyond even the dreams of the prophets, so that the situation could be described in only one way: "The Word was made flesh and dwelt among us". The fulfilment was so complete that it compelled this utterance as its only possible definition. The logic of the position here adopted involves our saying also that because He fulfils all that God had revealed of His own mind, will, purpose and nature under the Old Covenant, we affirm Jesus Christ to be the unique and supreme Revelation of God. It is not being said simply that in order to *understand* the Revelation of God in Jesus Christ it is necessary to interpret Him in Old Testament categories—as if the question were only an epistemological one. Rather is the position this, that the Revelation of God in Jesus Christ stands in an objective relation of fulfilment to the revelation given to Israel.

Our purpose at present is not to set forth a complete Christology, but in order to prepare for our further employment of the category of Incarnation the following comments may be made upon the relation of the idea of fulfilment to Christology: (i) The primacy of the idea of fulfilment both in the mind of Christ and in the New Testament Church has not been reflected in the historical creeds. Admittedly it appears in the theological background to the Creeds, for example, in the early Apologists, in Athanasius (particularly in *de Incarnatione*, c. VI), in St. Augustine and so on. But one would have expected it to be written into the very body of the Creeds if it were part of the original situation in which Jesus Christ was recognised in all His fullness. The fundamental question, therefore, which must be put to such a creed as the Chalcedonian Symbol, is whether it is integrated with a metaphysic which is alien to the idea of fulfilment, a metaphysic, in fact, which is static and rigid and too substantialist. (ii) It is highly probable that the restoration to its rightful place, in Christological statement, of the idea of fulfilment will come only with the full working out of what has earlier been called a metaphysic of history. Yet this is not quite a precise account of the matter, for, as we shall see, it is the idea or the category of Incarnation in the form of fulfilment which will be basic to the Christian metaphysic of history. At any rate, the idea of fulfilment will be more at home in a metaphysic of which it is prescriptive than in one which in most of its forms is antihistorical. (iii) The reinstatement of the idea of fulfilment in the Christological reference might lead to a reassessment of the contemporary emphasis on the description of Christ as "Revelation". As employed by some, this description tends to ignore the idea of fulfilment; and by others it is taken almost as a substitute for it. While the saner exponents of Revelation do not go to such extremes, nevertheless doubts remain whether they have done sufficient justice to the transition from speaking of Christ as fulfilment to speaking of Him as Revelation; or whether they have taken sufficient trouble to see that all the peculiar insights associated with the idea of fulfilment are safeguarded in their theology of Revelation.

The validation, however, of these general claims which are here made for the fuller recognition of the idea of fulfilment in Christological statement, and for the importance of this aspect of the category of Incarnation in the doctrine of history, can only properly rest on a detailed analysis of what fulfilment actually involves. To this end I propose to set forth what have been considered by certain previous writers on this subject as instances of ways in which Christ has been thought to "fulfil" certain events that preceded Him; and, consequently, to elicit through the examination of these instances what the pattern of fulfilment is. The writers here selected are :

(1) John Marsh: *The Fulness of Time*;
(2) A. G. Hebert: *The Throne of David*;
(3) R. Mackintosh: Article on "Fulfilment" in *The Dictionary of Christ and The Gospel*, Vol. I, pp. 626-29;
(4) Rudolf Bultmann: *Essays Philosophical and Theological*, E.T.

(1) No one can rightly orient himself nowadays in the complicated field of the problems associated with fulfilment except by reference to the very competent treatment of the subject by Dr. John Marsh.

Without, I trust, doing any violence to Dr. Marsh's exposition, I shall first set down the "fulfilment" situations which he selects from the New Testament evidence, and, secondly, deal with what he considers to be the structure of the fulfilment thus illustrated.

While admitting that there are many "strands" in the Old Testament which Jesus Christ was consciously aware of fulfilling, in addition to others mentioned by the Evangelists, the originality of which in the mind of Christ is difficult to determine (p. 98), Dr. Marsh regards three of these "strands" as dominant: "the account of the Exodus, the description of the Suffering Servant, and certain psalms" (p. 84). The Baptism of Jesus is related in detail to the original Exodus situation: the new Israel in the one Person of Jesus Christ having come out of Egypt (Matt. 2.15) must pass through the new Red Sea of baptism, before being ready for the New Covenant. Jesus is next submitted to the Temptations in the desert, corresponding to the trials endured by the old Israel in the wilderness. He gave to His followers His Sermon on the Mount, as Moses had given to his people the Torah on Mount Sinai. Christ presented Himself to His disciples as their Shepherd, calling to mind no doubt the way in which Moses and Aaron had led the old Israel (Ps. 77.20). Christ called and appointed Twelve Apostles, and sent out seventy disciples, thus fulfilling in them the purpose of the Twelve Tribes, and the seventy elders who shared responsibility with Moses. The Crucifixion of Christ was associated by St. Paul with the Exodus, when he spoke of it as a Passover in which Christ was sacrificed for us. But the part which the idea of fulfilment played in Christ's understanding of His mission in Israel is to be illustrated also from His use of the Suffering Servant theme—if not of actual quotations from the Servant Songs—at His Baptism; in the parable of the wicked husbandmen; in His disclosure to Peter, James and John before the Transfiguration that the Messiah "must suffer many things"; and finally in His discourse to the disciples at Emmaus on the necessity for His Death. The third strand of fulfilment which Dr. Marsh chooses is that of the Psalms, the examples being drawn from the week of the Passion—Ps. 118.22,23 being used at Mk. 12.10,11; Ps. 110.1 at Lk. 20.42,43, when Christ wishes to validate His own authority; Ps. 41.9 when He foretells, during the Last Supper, that one of the disciples will betray Him; Ps. 22.1, Ps. 31.5, forming the basis of the words from the Cross.

Before proceeding to the second part of our exposition of Dr. Marsh's account of fulfilment, we may make the following

observations on the evidence thus submitted. In view of the
fact that Dr. Marsh deals in great detail with each of these
three strands—he rightly does so—and also because of the
limits imposed upon him both by the theme of this chapter,
"The Accepted Time", and by the general thesis of his book,
he has to make certain omissions. Some of those are here
mentioned, because they may turn out to be of importance
when we examine the rest of Dr. Marsh's treatment of
fulfilment.

(i) When Dr. Marsh deals with Christ's relation to the
Torah (p. 85), he interprets it, as we have seen, within the
Exodus pattern. But he does not refer to Mt. 5.17, where
Christ, after denying that He has come to destroy the law and
the prophets, explicitly states that He has come to fulfil. Now
admittedly there are difficulties in this verse. For example,
the second sentence in it, "I came not to destroy but to fulfil",
may be a general saying, without a known specific context,
which has been attached by the Evangelist to Christ's statement
about destroying "the law and the prophets". Or, again,
the original saying may have been a denial of Christ's intention
to destroy the prophets, but because of the traditional use of
the phrase "the law and the prophets", the original saying
was expanded to include the law—though this suggestion
really does not carry any great weight; in other parts of the
Sermon on the Mount, Christ does oppose His "I say unto
you" to the "Ye have heard it said", and it is the law that is in
question. There nevertheless remain the problems of deciding,
first, whether Christ's hearers would understand Him to fulfil
the law in the same sense in which He fulfilled the prophets;
and, secondly, whether we can discern some difference in the
notion of fulfilment in the two connections. The immediate
point of interest in relation to Dr. Marsh's treatment of the
Sermon on the Mount as fulfilment of part of the Exodus
pattern is that Mt. 5.17 does not quite fit into such a pattern.
Dr. J. Y. Campbell (*A Theological Word Book of the Bible*,
edited by A. Richardson, p. 88) interprets Mt. 5.17 to mean
that Jesus Christ, by His teaching, brings the law to completion
and brings out its full intention.

(ii) The question might be raised whether, once one form

of the Messianic category ("The Suffering Servant") is introduced in illustration of the idea of fulfilment, the other two,
which are equally important, namely, "Son of God" and "Son
of Man", do not claim *equal* attention.   Now Dr. Marsh does,
of course, mention both of these Messianic categories, as we
should expect him to do, but the position would seem to be
somewhat more complex than is suggested by simply putting
the three groups of Messianic ideas side by side.   Is it not
rather this, that Jesus fulfilled the Messianic promise of the
Old Testament, and that He did so according to the three
forms of the Messianic category?   That is, we can speak of
Jesus as Messianic fulfilment only in terms of these three
concepts; and Messianic fulfilment is not to be described or
even discussed apart from these forms of the Messianic
category.

(iii) No doubt Dr. Marsh would agree with Professor
C. H. Dodd's statement that "the New Testament writers
. . . do not attempt to exploit the whole corpus of Messianic
prediction" (*History and the Gospel*, p. 61); yet surely any
account of fulfilment requires, for completeness, to include
realisation of expectations.   This is a matter to which we shall
be obliged to return in discussing "the form" of fulfilment,
and yet, though the New Testament writers could have woven
the notion of national leader, king, and even judge, into the
pattern of prediction which Christ realised, the fact that they
did not is no proof that for them, at least, part of the fulfilment
which Jesus accomplished was fulfilment of prediction.   And
this kind of situation, therefore, must be regarded as evidence
in the collection of situations regarded by New Testament
writers as "fulfilment" situations.

To turn now to Dr. Marsh's analysis of "the form" of
fulfilment as distinct from the content, we observe that he
makes a preliminary negative analysis, and then proceeds to
show us four positive forms of the idea of fulfilment.   He
begins by rejecting two possible interpretations of fulfilment
as applied to the person and work of Jesus Christ.   The first
is the naturalistic view which holds that in Jesus Christ there
came to final fruition some historical process whose natural
course of evolution could be followed in the Old Testament.

This view is wrong in that it contradicts the Biblical affirmation that what happens in Christ has a supernatural rather than a natural origin. The second view rejected by Dr. Marsh is one more commonly held by Christian interpreters of fulfilment, namely, that it involves nothing more than the imposing upon the events of the Life, Death and Resurrection of Jesus Christ of a certain pattern of occurrence discernible in certain Old Testament events. That is, it is false to suggest that "fulfilment" is a hermeneutical principle, convenient for our employment *now* in the understanding of Christ, but not integral to the fabric of Christ's Life, Death and Resurrection. And this view is false because Christ Himself spoke and acted according to the pattern indicated by certain Old Testament situations, for He believed Himself to be essentially related to them. We have already seen how extensively Dr. Marsh illustrates this position from the words and actions of Jesus Christ.

Dr. Marsh most helpfully presents to us three positive interpretations of the notion of fulfilment, and a fourth by implication. First, situation S_n may be said to fulfil situation S_a, if S_a has to be kept in mind for the understanding of S_n. S_a may take the form either of actual statements made (for example, by the Prophets) or of events, which are relevant to the "interpretation" of S_n. This analysis of fulfilment is different from the second one above which Dr. Marsh rejects in this respect that: whereas the previous view simply employed S_a as a convenient hermeneutical principle for understanding S_n, and so imposed on S_n a pattern which was not really essential or native to it, the present view maintains that, first, S_n is actually incomprehensible except in terms of S_a and that S_a is continued into S_n and is organic with it.

Secondly, situation S_n may be said to fulfil situation S_a when a word spoken by a true prophet in S_a, and having thereby acquired a "quasi-objective reality", actualises itself at S_n. This word spoken by a true prophet is identified both with the Word of God and with the purpose of God. This word or purpose, once it is uttered in S_a, carries in itself the power finally to become "ingredient", to use the language of Whitehead adopted by Dr. Marsh at this point, in an actual historical event. Obviously this view does not conflict with the first, but it does differ from the first in the following respects:

(i) that in the second view the point of reference is S_a and the direction of reference is S_a to S_n, while in the first view the point of reference is S_n and the direction of reference is S_n to S_a; and

(ii) that in the first view the analogy discerned between S_n and S_a is drawn only for purposes of description or understanding, while in the second view, there is a genuine *analogia entis* between S_n and S_a.

Thirdly, Dr. Marsh offers what is in effect a variant of the second view: S_n fulfils S_a whenever S_a signifies something which is accomplished perfectly in S_n. The example submitted is that of the Exodus, which signifies that God will save His people and is itself an incomplete embodiment of that purpose of God. This event all happens perfectly and completely in Jesus Christ, but more precisely, when as our Passover He is sacrificed for us, so that His Death is the fulfilment of the Exodus. On this view, *events* as well as prophecies have fulfilments: or, prophecies may be either words or events and both have fulfilments. Fourthly—though Dr. Marsh does not offer it as such—there is the suggestion (given in the exposition of Lk. 12.50) that in this third case the "fulfilment" of S_a by S_n may mean that S_n is the final member in a series of which S_a is the first member, "the last act which completes (the) process". It is justifiable to nominate this view as a fourth view, for it is distinguishable from the third in the following way. According to the third view S_a is regarded as an inadequate embodiment of a definable purpose of God, of which S_n is the perfect embodiment, while, in the fourth view, attention is drawn to the fact that S_n is the temporal end-term of a series.

(2) A. G. Hebert, in *The Throne of David*, particularly pp. 127-42—a work of which Dr. Marsh does not take account, though the two writings taken together provide an interesting comparison—sets down at the beginning of his exposition of fulfilment a very full statement of "the Christian Gospel in Old Testament language" (p. 128). (The separate articles are in fact quotations from the Old Testament made in the New

Testament, chiefly in the Book of the Acts.) This statement is given for two reasons. The first is that it provides us with some idea of how the Apostles used the Old Testament during "the first two decades after Pentecost". The quotations are grouped under such headings as: The God of Israel, Fulfilment of His Messianic Promises in Jesus, of the seed of David, Who Jesus is, His Crucifixion, His Resurrection, His Ascension, The Outpouring of the Spirit of the Lord, Warning to those who hear. The whole substance of the Gospel Message, in other words, could be stated in Old Testament language. The second reason determining Dr. Hebert's presentation of the Gospel in this language is that by so doing he is able to make clear the basic structure of the New Testament message, as being that of promise-fulfilment. The life and mission of Jesus Christ are to be understood only if they are related to the totality of the Messianic hope which is *the* burden of the Old Testament. Dr. Hebert does not mean that this promise-fulfilment category is a convenient principle of interpretation, to be discarded if some other more useful or more modern one happens along; on the contrary, it is because He stands in this line of promise-fulfilment that Jesus is "who He is". This is not to deny that He stands where He does because He is who He is: but it *is* to deny that He can be removed from this line and remain the Jesus of whom the Bible speaks. To make his position quite precise, on the negative side at least, Dr. Hebert denies that this group of quotations presenting the New Testament message in Old Testament terms is either a collection of resemblances of literary interest only, or a group of predictions specifically validated by actual occurrences in the Life and Death of Jesus Christ. On the positive side, the position maintained is that these quotations are to be regarded as the means by which the Person and Work of Jesus Christ are to be interpreted.

Dr. Hebert develops his theme by outlining the precise lines of fulfilment which exhibit "a clear continuity of theological principle" (p. 130): (*a*) that which deals with the promised King who should reign on David's throne, anointed with the Spirit of Jehovah ; (*b*) that presenting a Prophet like unto Moses to whom the people shall listen; and (*c*) the

E

whole Servant of Jehovah theme, in particular. The comparison with the fulfilment strands chosen by Dr. Marsh is interesting: they both agree on the Suffering Servant theme and the use of the Psalms in interpreting the Messiahship of Christ, and even the concept of Kingship emphasised by Dr. Hebert has its place in Dr. Marsh's presentation. It is, however, the emphasis laid upon the Exodus theme, his employment of it as, one might say, the key to all else, which distinguishes Dr. Marsh from the earlier writer.

To bring our examination of Dr. Hebert's analysis of fulfilment into line with the previous direction of our discussion, we may say that he suggests several possible interpretations of the concept, not all of which he accepts:

(i) Situation S_n may be said to fulfil situation S_a when, because of certain analogies, some of an interesting nature, features of S_a are useful in the description of S_n (rejected). (ii) S_n fulfils S_a when in S_n there is evidence that events predicted in detail in S_a actually come to pass (rejected). (iii) S_n fulfils S_a when the latter provides certain concepts without which S_n does not "make sense"; or when S_n compels for its adequate interpretation the use of concepts to be found only in S_a (accepted). (iv) A severe critic might say that iii is only a refined form of i, and the criticism can only be averted by the addition of a fourth sense of the concept of fulfilment to which Dr. Hebert virtually alludes when he speaks about "lines of development" and "clear continuity of theological principle" (p. 130). In this sense, S_n fulfils S_a when they can be shown to be joined by a line of development in such a way that S_n embodies the accomplishment of something proposed in S_a; or S_n embodies completely some principle only partially embodied in S_a. It is because of this continuity of development that S_n requires S_a for its interpretation (sense iii). The question remains, of course, whether you can have sense iv without importing into it something of the element of prediction and verification of actual detail (sense ii).

One other section of Dr. Hebert's treatment of fulfilment may be noted at this stage, namely, his analysis (footnote, op. cit., pp. 137 ff.) of the differences between this expectation and the fulfilment, which he holds to be twofold. First, the

Person of the Messiah leaps into the foreground in the fulfilment related in the New Testament, having held a minor rôle
since I Isaiah. The Person of the Messiah now, as it were, fills
the whole sphere of the Kingdom of God, all the promises of
the latter being contained in Him and its duties exhausted in
loyalty to Him, and to Him crucified. Secondly, in the fulfilment it is realised, as was not the case in the time of expectation,
that the Messianic Kingdom consists of "two stages, two
spheres, two levels: a Present and a Future, an Imperfect
and a Perfect; an Earthly and a Heavenly" (p. 139)—which I
take to be Dr. Hebert's way of saying that there are elements
of truth both in realised and in consistent eschatology. The
actual content of the differences between the expectation and
the fulfilment is a matter yet to be considered: it is sufficient
at the moment to note that the existence of such differences is a
refutation of the simple prediction-verification interpretation
of fulfilment.

(3) R. Mackintosh (*Dictionary of Christ and The Gospels*,
Vol. I, pp. 626-29). Following our previous division into
content and form, we find that for Dr. Mackintosh the content
of fulfilment consists of three groups of evidence, namely, the
three lines of expectation which are fulfilled in Christ: (i)
Israel's hope of a Messianic King (Is. 9); (ii) the hope of God's
own coming to His people in person (Is. 40.10; Is. 40-45
generally), a hope pointing to the Deity of Christ; and (iii)
the expectation in the Suffering Servant (Is. 52.13 to the end of
c. 53) which anticipated the Passion of Christ. This material
illustrative of the fulfilment theme is very similar in its first
and last groupings to elements in the material submitted by
Dr. Marsh and Dr. Hebert. Dr. Mackintosh is unique among
the three writers contemplated at present in his contention
that the Incarnation is anticipated in the Old Testament;
but he would be at pains to validate his contention with any
hope of conclusiveness from the evidence he submits.

It is in reference to the "form" of fulfilment that Dr.
Mackintosh has his most interesting remarks to make. He
discovers the following senses: (i) Following Bertholet's
comment on Ezr. 1.1 = II Chr. 36.22, he quotes the view that
fulfilment takes place when a prophetic word once spoken,

and thus entered "among the powers of the real world", gradually accomplishes itself. Not until the actual accomplishment contains all that the prophetic word promised has fulfilment taken place. This view is identical with that to which Dr. Marsh referred when he spoke of the prophetic word acquiring "quasi-objective reality". Fulfilment on this reading is the end-term in a process which is reached by a continuous quantitative growth. (ii) Dr. Mackintosh places in sharp opposition to the former view one which he regards as the authentic New Testament conception of fulfilment, namely, that fulfilment occurs "in detailed mechanical correspondence with the letter of prediction". The fact that God in the Old Testament has said that a certain event might happen to Christ is prescriptive of its occurrence. Dr. Mackintosh here openly contends for a view which Dr. Marsh and Dr. Hebert allowed only with the severest limitations.

CHAPTER SIX

HISTORY AND THE INCARNATION

(*a*) THE INCARNATION AS FULFILMENT (*contd.*)

Rudolf bultmann, "Prophecy and Fulfilment" (pp. 182-208, *Essays*, E.T.). It is not surprising that R. Bultmann, having stated his criticisms of the views expressed so variously by the above writers, should endeavour to take up a position right outside of all of them. The extent of his rejection of these views and the satisfactoriness of his own position are our next immediate subjects of consideration. In the New Testament and in the tradition of the Church, we are told that "prophecy is understood to be the forecasting of a future happening, and fulfilment is the occurrence of what has been forecast " (op. cit., p. 182). Bultmann discerns a double truth in this understanding of the matter. On the one hand, when the Jewish tradition of the Old Testament is followed, the New Testament regards the prophecies of the Old Testament prophets as referring to the eschatological age of salvation. On the other hand, when the New Testament treats the whole of the Old Testament as a book of prophecy, and reads a Messianic interpretation into texts not so intended by the original writers, then the New Testament is in line with the stoic tradition of rather artificial allegorising. After a detailed examination of both prophetic and what he calls "random" passages of the Old Testament used by the New Testament writers, he becomes very specific in the statement of his reasons for rejecting this kind of interpretation of prophecy and fulfilment.

(i) First of all, this way of using the Old Testament has become impossible in an age which approaches the book with methods of modern historical science. What is meant by this rather succinct dismissal of a very long-respected position is that the Old Testament prophet would be thinking and speaking of events, and more particularly of a person, quite different from those in which the New Testament found the

61

fulfilment of the prophecy. That is, if at a time t_a A B is speaking of C D, then historical science will not permit W X to affirm at time t_x that "really" A B was speaking about Y Z.

(ii) Instances may be cited in which the "fulfilment" can only be maintained by the actual misconstruction of the Old Testament text. For example, Is. 7.14 becomes a prophetic text concerning the Virgin birth for Mt. 1.23 only because the Hebrew *Almah* is translated as παρθένος. Ps. 78, which is used at Mt. 13.35 as a proof of Jesus' speaking in parables, is not a prophetic Psalm.

(iii) Bultmann discerns an apologetic purpose in the whole use of prophecies by the Primitive Church. Through their use, by demonstrating the necessity of the Death of Christ and the character of His Death in terms of certain forecasts, the Church hoped to break down the scandal of Christ's Passion for Jews and Gentiles alike. The premise in such apologetic was that the Death of Christ would appear to be less "objectionable and astonishing" if it were presented as "predestined and prophesied". In terms of his well-known Christian existentialism, Bultmann points out that the scandal of Christ's death cannot be broken down, even although it is demonstrated that it was necessitated by certain forecasts; and he implies by his use of the rhetorical question that the scandal can be overcome only by grasping its "meaning and significance".

(iv) The more general charge is made that this whole process of discovering prophecies in the Old Testament which "prove" the validity of the claims of Christ involves a very arbitrary and subjective standard of selection. Bultmann groups the New Testament use of the Old Testament with the extravagances of some of the Fathers of the Church, who established very fanciful analogies between the work of Christ and events and things in the Old Testament. His main point is that there is no control properly exercised either in the New Testament or in the tradition of the Church over this use of prophecy, nor can he rightly see how such control could be established.

In the next section of the article Bultmann criticises a

view held by J. C. K. Hofmann in his *Prophecy and Fulfilment*,
namely, that it is the history of Israel rather than the
words of the Old Testament which are prophetic of the coming
of Christ. Christ appears within history as the goal or fulfilment of a movement which has across the centuries been
gradually leading up to Himself. Hofmann had apparently
enlarged the bounds of the history thus prophetic to include
that of the whole world in general. Bultmann's reply here is
that such a theory as Hofmann's is committed to a philosophy
of history predominantly Hegelian, and one which is Christian-
ised only because Hofmann has identified Christ with the goal
of history. He further involves Hofmann in the self-stulti-
fication of saying that Christ must first be recognised as the
goal of history before Israel's history can be interpreted as
moving to this goal. If not, then Hofmann would be using
a secular philosophy of history and of Israel's history to prove
the validity of Christ.

It is rather interesting that prior to establishing his own
view of the nature of prophecy and fulfilment, and as evidence
for it, Bultmann should employ a method similar to that of the
writers whom we have previously considered. That is, he submits to us instances of prophecy-fulfilment, what we have
previously called the "content of fulfilment", and proceeds
thereafter to extract the "form" or "structure" of fulfilment.
He selects three concepts in the Old Testament which the New
Testament employs for the demonstration of the claim that
Christ is the fulfilment of the Old Testament, and he shows
that the New Testament interprets them in what he calls "a
new sense—that is eschatologically". These three concepts
are as follows:

(i) *The Covenant Concept.* Bultmann's method in his
interpretation of the concept of Covenant is to demonstrate
that there is a contradiction at its heart. On the one hand, in the
Old Testament the Covenant is spoken of as if it were a con-
tract between God and a definite historical entity, the people
of God. This Covenant serves when the idea of election is
employed, to distinguish the "Chosen People" from the
Gentiles. On the other hand there are constant protests against
the suggestion that God's bond with His people is irrevocable

and that the Covenant is in itself a ground of permanent security either for the people or for the individuals in Israel. Along this line the prophets contend that the Covenant between God and His people stands only so long as individual Israelites obey God's moral demands. The people of God on such an interpretation is not an empirical group and God's Covenant is an eschatological concept. In the same way, in the New Testament, the eschatological nature of the concept of Covenant is demonstrated in the fact that the new community inaugurated in the Death of Christ is not a historical body, nor is it bound to the world. In fact the New Covenant takes its members out of the world.

(ii) *The Concept of the Kingdom of God.* Bultmann refers to the twofold idea in Israel's history of the Kingship of God as being both present and future, the former emphasising the Lordship of Yahweh, imposing His will upon the people now, dispensing justice amongst them, and generally protecting them; the latter, developing in the time of the Exile, projecting the establishment of God's Kingdom into the future, and investing it with political qualities. In the preaching of Jesus, however, both of these aspects are rejected, and the "Kingdom of God" comes to mean the dominion of God over a community in which the Sermon on the Mount is God's will for His people and where His name is ever hallowed. The Kingdom in this sense, that is, the community in which God realises His rule, is now, because Christ has been made King through His resurrection. Such an eschatological interpretation of the Kingdom of God is discontinuous with both the Old Testament expectations.

(iii) *The Concept of the People of God.* While there had been in the days of the Kings a tension between the idea that Israel has but one King, namely God, and the actual historical existence of an earthly King organising a secular state, with its army, taxation and foreign politics, after the Exile, with the disappearance of the secular state of Israel, the theocratic conception naturally gained great strength. Nevertheless, the Jewish people remains an historical entity, distinguishable from other people by empirical characteristics, and they retain their expectation of the recovery of their historical nationhood.

Bultmann, at this point, again emphasises the contradiction between the idea of a People of God under His royal dominion and the people as a secular state. The New Testament, which affirms that the new aeon has come in Christ, discovers the People of God present in the Christian community. Access to this community comes through response to the Gospel's call and through baptism.

When Bultmann crystallises his conclusions from this analysis of the content of fulfilment, he affirms the category of prophecy-fulfilment in a quite unique way. Prophecy is fulfilled in what he calls "its inner contradiction, its miscarriage". Prophecy is fulfilled, in other words, in that it is not fulfilled. In each of the three concepts discussed above, those of the Covenant, of the Kingdom of God, of the People of God, he detects a contradiction between an empirical historical situation to which the prophecy in each case refers, and an eschatological idea unrealisable within the world. It is to this contradiction that Bultmann refers when he speaks about the "miscarriage of history". History, as it were, held within it a certain promise which we may designate prophecy, promise concerning certain empirical historical situations which were to come to pass. In the "fulfilment" something of a different order eventuates, this order being called eschatological. At an earlier point in this article (op. cit., p. 191) Bultmann had said that, according to the New Testament, Christ is the end of salvation history, not as a culmination of its historical development, but because He is its eschatological end. Historical development brings man to the point at which he realises that he cannot attain to eternal significance of life. It is only when he "encounters the Grace of God", and is abstracted by God from the world, that he receives the possibility of faith, and with it the new eschatological existence in the world and in time.

Bultmann's position is still, however, slightly more complex. Up to date we have been interpreting him as saying that the failure of history to realise its true end is the miscarriage of the promise contained in history. This miscarriage is seen most clearly in the field of the three concepts discussed by Bultmann. The further thing which Bultmann is saying is that this very history of miscarriage is itself a promise, namely, that God will lead His people by some other way to that existence which is their proper end. The Faith which God gives as the way of entering into eschatological existence has constantly to become aware that events in a secular sphere are not identifiable with those in the eschatological.

Such then is Bultmann's analysis of the category of history which we are investigating. Some initial comments may be made about the analysis in general. The complete divergence from the views which we have previously examined is patent, Bultmann rejecting them all in one comprehensive gesture. It is clear, too, that the customary percentage of the iceberg is not observable, for much of what Bultmann has to say rests upon premises that are nowhere stated, and upon definitions which he does not have the opportunity to give us. How much simpler—if also how much less intriguing—the whole article would be if he had explained his use of the term "eschatological". Incidentally, the article is much more relevant to our study of the doctrine of history than might at first appear, on two counts. First, the agnosticism concerning world history, and the disavowal of philosophy of history which goes with it, are in fact a form of philosophy of history, and express some kind of basic metaphysic of history, or at least some suspicion that there is something there to talk about and that most people talk about it in the wrong way. Secondly, Bultmann draws attention to the point which Dr. Marsh accepted rather unquestioningly, that the fact that Christ is the goal of salvation history is *not* equivalent to His being the goal of world history. On the other hand, the article raises many problems in regard to Bultmann's general theological position which it is impossible to discuss in this setting. For example, the precise meaning, as above mentioned, of the term "eschatological", which is such a problem in his other writings, escapes detection in this essay. Without attempting to compare usage, we may observe that in the present work the word is variously applied to (i) concepts (Covenant, People of God, and so on) and in this connection it is antithesised to empirical, historical, and seems to mean that which is beyond history (as on p. 199, 2 lines from foot of page); (ii) the activity of God (p. 207), when God withdraws man from the world and instals him in the new order of existence which is known as the eschatological (which is a reversion to sense i); (iii) the attitude of faith, which discerns through encounter with the grace of God the eternal significance of human existence. Another important matter of general interest in Bultmann's work which is here relevant is what exactly he means by history, and *Heilsgeschichte*, and how these two are related to one another. Both this subject and the one previously mentioned bear directly on the whole theme of the essay, but the most tantalising feature of the essay is that while it raises these questions it does not provide anything like sufficient evidence for answering them. We shall therefore in our examination of Bultmann's analysis of prophecy and fulfilment confine ourselves to the more specific topics raised therein and refer to these larger issues only when absolutely necessary.

(i) Bultmann's discussion brings out very clearly one feature of the prophecy-fulfilment category which the other writers so far examined have not mentioned. It is this, that the category of prophecy-fulfilment may have one function in the Primitive Church and a rather different function in the modern Church. The question left in our minds, of course, is whether Bultmann is speaking of the same category as that employed by the Primitive Church, or whether he has not in fact introduced something quite new. At any rate for the present he puts us on our guard against over-rationalising the use made by the Primitive Church of prophecy-fulfilment. In fact, Bultmann's analysis does offer one solution to the seeming contradiction between the views of Dr. Marsh and those of Dr. Mackintosh: the former, in his elaborate and analogical analysis of the place of the Exodus pattern in prophecy-fulfilment, could be said to be offering the kind of interpretation which has "meaning and significance" for a generation which has rediscovered the "unity" of the Bible, whereas the latter is remaining more faithful in a scientific historical way to the majority of the Old and New Testament prophecies and fulfilments.

(ii) Bultmann's own revision of the content and form of the prophecy-fulfilment category springs from what I would regard as a false proposition concerning the use of that category in the Primitive Church, and from a false premise in preparation for his own interpretation. First of all he says that the use of prophecy was designed to reduce the scandal of the Gospel; that is, it was an argument used to establish a Gospel which could somehow be separated from the argument. As we have already seen, if we are going to use the phrase "the argument from prophecy" in this connection, then we must emphasise that the "argument" is part of the *kerugma* and not in any way isolable from it. On the contrary, the purpose of the use of prophecy-fulfilment by the New Testament writers, and indeed by the formulators of the oral tradition, was to supply the only terms in which the Person and Work of Jesus Christ could be properly understood. As a result, the interpretation of Christ in this way may have reduced "the scandal", but it is very doubtful whether the New Testament writers ever expected to remove it; St. Paul certainly never did. Bultmann is rather unjust when he judges the New Testament use of prophecy-fulfilment by the rather fantastic use which some of the Apostolic Fathers make of the category later. Clement's interpretation of Rahab's scarlet cord is scarcely a very good standard by which to judge, say, the New Testament's use of Is. 53 in the interpretation of the Death of Christ. No theological idea can ever fairly be judged by its worst exponents, nor is a theological method to be condemned because some people have abused it.

(iii) Having discarded the material by which the New Testament writers generally interpreted the Person and Work of Jesus Christ, Bultmann does not offer us any alternative canon of interpretation. If Christ is not interpreted as the fulfilment of prophecy, that being the original description of Him, how then are we to describe Him? Or, to put the question in the language which he himself uses: how are we to determine the meaning and significance of Jesus Christ? It is no answer to this question to say that, in fact, Bultmann does use the prophecy-fulfilment category; for his examination of the three concepts, which might yield the normal form of the prophecy-fulfilment category, yields quite negative results. It is quite clear that there is no answer within the bounds of this essay to the problem of the criterion which Bultmann employs to determine the content of the Christian Gospel.

(iv) We may look for a moment at the details of a sentence which sums up a good deal of what Bultmann is saying. Christ is the end of *Heilsgeschichte* because He is its eschatological end. This he regards as a legitimate form of the affirmation of the prophecy-fulfilment category. As far as I can judge it is either a tautological statement, or it is guilty of the logical confusion with which Bultmann himself charges all statements, that Christ is the goal of world history. The criticism of tautology might be substantiated in this way. Salvation history is that kind of history which has an eschatological end. Indeed, this is what makes it salvation history. So, to say that Christ is the end of salvation history is to say that He is its eschatological end. This criticism is not as facile as it may at first appear, for Bultmann, when he makes this point (p. 191), is attempting to show that Christ's claim to be the end of salvation history does not rest upon the fact that He is the goal of all historical developments. As for the logical confusion, on the other hand, Christ must first of all be recognised as the end of salvation history before the "course" of salvation history can be plotted; or, to put it in other words, it is only when the eschatological end is known that its precursors in salvation history can be recognised. The alternative to this way of describing the matter would be one which Bultmann himself would have to reject, namely, that the end of salvation history was something that was known before Christ came, and that at His coming He was identified with this end.

(v) When I come to the more positive elements in Bultmann's analysis of the prophecy-fulfilment category, I find it difficult to determine which of two positions the more correctly reflects his mind. (*a*) On the one hand, we may begin with his statement (p. 191) that the three concepts (Covenant, Kingdom of God, People of God) are picked up by the New Testament out of the Old and interpreted in a new way (eschatologically). There is then continuity between the Old and New Testaments along the line of these three concepts, the New Testament substituting its interpretation for the less mature in the Old Testament. It could almost be said that the Old Testament predicts that there will be, for example, a New Covenant, a Kingdom and a people, even although it is mistaken about the characteristics which each of the three will bear. It was right about the *that* but it was wrong about the *how*. But the fact that the New Testament can still refer to each of the three concepts instead of using some completely different terms implies that what the Old Testament said was not entirely false.

(*b*) On the other hand, Bultmann states that there is an inner contradiction in Hebrew prophecy which makes it impossible of fulfilment, miscarriage being the other term that he uses of the situation. Now it is possible that he could mean, by this sentence, that in Hebrew prophecy we have *A* and *Not-A*, and that when the prophecy is fulfilled, there is genuine continuity, "carry over" into the fulfilment situation, *A* being the medium of continuity. *Not-A*, not being carried over, is not fulfilled; in other words, it "miscarries". But that this is not the whole of what Bultmann intends, by any means, is clear from the fact that he wishes to regard the contradiction, the miscarriage, as the situation which the fulfilment fulfils. That is, it is the conflict of *A* with *Not-A* which is prophetic. The result then is that fulfilment is so called because in fact it does not fulfil. It comes rather as a kind of Hegelian synthesis of the thesis and antithesis which were contained in Old Testament prophecy—though Bultmann would violently reject the comparison. Such an interpretation of Bultmann perhaps over-rationalises what he is trying to say, for in the Hegelian synthesis there is embodied the truth of both thesis and antithesis, whereas Bultmann's synthesis is not so accommodating, for it negates both. The failure of both elements in the contradiction at the heart of Old Testament prophecy is the expectation which anticipates the fulfilment.

Bultmann's conception of the miscarriage of prophecy forms a very adequate introduction to an aspect of the notion of fulfilment to which scant justice has been done by the other writers so far discussed, namely, the polarity of fulfilment. According to this notion, fulfilment has two poles, positive and negative, so that fulfilment stands in this double relation to prophecy of both affirming it and denying it. What in fact happens is that fulfilment affirms certain aspects of the prophetic message and denies other parts, but the affirmation and the negation are so interwoven that it is impossible to establish any point-to-point correlation between the confirmation and what is confirmed, or between the negation and what is negated. It is therefore impossible to save the confirmation and throw away the negation; both are necessary parts in the polarity of fulfilment. It is the polarity of fulfilment which ultimately prevents us from making a decision between the notion of fulfilment as realisation of anticipation and the notion of it as being more complete expression of a certain pattern of Divine behaviour. Bultmann, on the other hand, sees polarity only in prophecy, failing to realise that it can be affirmed there only on the basis of the polarity of fulfilment. Prophecy by itself contains no contradiction; fulfilment could be said to do so, but the notion of polarity is a more accurate description. Bultmann commits the second error of thinking that the notion of polarity can be eliminated from fulfilment, so that in the end he has a fulfilment which stands in no organic relation whatsoever to the prophecy which it fulfils. That, in fact, is not an unjust assessment of his conclusion, and it amounts to a conception of fulfilment which has no longer any connection with the regular use of the term.

Since, therefore, fulfilment is one—in fact, the original—way of describing the Incarnation, the polarity which we ascribe to the one may be affirmed of the other. The example which readily springs to mind is "ethic of Jesus" as it is stated in the Sermon on the Mount. On the one hand, there is Our Lord's assurance that one jot and one tittle of the Law shall not pass away till all be fulfilled—His affirmation of anticipation of His own Law in the old Law. On the other hand, we have His forthright statement: "It has been said unto you of old, but I say unto you. . . ." The Biblical critics may one day resolve the polarity contained in the contrariness of these two positions, but they seem to me to be so embedded in the very essence of Incarnation and fulfilment that the critics may be seeking the impossible in endeavouring to reconcile them, or dispose of the one in favour of the other. Another example would be the relation in which Jesus stands to the Messianic hopes of Old Israel. In this relation are present both negative and positive poles; Christ affirms some of these hopes and rejects others. I do not simply mean that he rejected the idea of a political leader who would set Israel in a position of world dominance, and that he accepted the Isaianic Suffering Servant, but that within the rejection of the first there is some affirmation—He it is by whom kings rule and princes decree justice—that he is the Lord of politics; and within the second there is some negation—denial of the separateness of God from the Servant. So too, the Death of Christ stands under the same canon of bi-polar interpretation. As spoken of by Himself and as understood by St. Paul and the others, the Death of Christ shows points of affinity with the Old Testament conception of how salvation would come to Israel: the late Professor Donald Baillie has shown how the two strands of free forgiveness and forgiveness at a great price, both existing in the Old Testament, become united in one in the New Testament presentation of the Atonement. At the same time a reading of the Epistle to the Hebrews soon illustrates the extent to which Old Testament conceptions are discarded, even when they are integral to the strands that are affirmed.

Having in this way maintained the necessity of the negative pole in the conception of fulfilment, let me make the three following comments on it:

(i) The recognition of this negative pole is in effect an admission of the gap that must exist between prophecy and fulfilment, between anticipation and realisation of God's promises. There is in the fulfilment a novelty which is the expression of Divine grace, far beyond man's expectations. The loss of the sense of novelty is the greatest single obstacle preventing modern man from appreciating the relevance of the challenge of Christ. So there is no greater responsibility upon us who are called to preach the Gospel in the Advent season than to try, under God's mercy, to recreate by our preaching this lost sense of wonder. It is a curious irony that in the beginning it was this very novelty of the Incarnation which prevented the religious leaders of Israel from apprehending who Jesus really was. Following the prophecies, for we must give them their due, they could see no connection between this Christ and Him whom their prophecies led them to expect.

(ii) In the history of thought concerning the Incarnation and fulfilment it is interesting to note the ways in which the negative pole has at times been over-emphasised, and again under-emphasised, or even neglected. The negation appears in the Epistles of the Apostle Paul, coming out in his very severe strictures upon the Law, which worketh sin and death. Marcion observed this same negation with all the myopia and tenacity of the heretic. But this kind of emphasis is not confined to the early Church ; it seems always to have had a place somewhere in Christian theology. It appears in some Lutheran accounts of the relation of Church and State; in the "two morality" theories of those Pietists who deny to the Christian ethic of love any relevance to the evil world in which Christians have to live their daily lives; in the rejection of apologetics as a valid theological discipline, and so on.

But the negative pole in fulfilment has been just as much neglected as over-emphasised in historical theology: for example, by those who have prematurely identified the Christian ethic with contemporary conventionalities; by those who entertain delusions of "Christianising" society; by those who think that the sole task of Christian theology is either natural theology (the Deists) or apologetics, and tend to deny that dogmatics is an obligatory discipline for the Church, so that she may speak to herself, without worrying or wondering whether the world hears or not, about God, the Father, the Son and the Holy Spirit, who is her Lord and Saviour, as He is not that of the world. But the negation is more subtly forgotten by those Biblical scholars who seem to regard the Old Testament almost as a series of proof-texts for the New Testament. Now, in all truth, I have no time for the people who look on the Old Testament as a collection of tribal myths or even as a primer for the new depth-psychology; nevertheless, I do not think that we necessarily do the Old Testament any service nor do we correctly represent its relation to the New Testament if we regard the unity of the Bible as that of a system of co-ordinate parts. It is true that the Old and the New Testaments

F

both witness to the great central fact of the coming of the Messiah, but we dare never forget that they witness to it in quite different ways, the one by speaking prophetically as not yet having received the promises, the other kerygmatically as having entered into the fulfilment. The unity of the Bible is then of this very peculiar sort in which the component parts do not stand on an equal footing. The recognition of the negative pole in fulfilment is a safeguard against any premature or superficial assessments of the unity of the Bible.

(iii) The primacy of the concept of fulfilment over that of Revelation as the original description of the Incarnate Lord, coupled with the ineradicable presence in the concept of fulfilment of the negative pole, makes me ask the question whether we do not have here, if not a solution, at least a preferable restatement of an honoured theological problem, namely that of special and general revelation. This problem as normally understood is as follows: Through special revelation, we know propositions s_{a-m} (the Old Testament) and s_{n-x} (the New Testament) concerning God; while according to general revelation we know propositions g_{a-m}. Do any of the latter propositions coincide with any of the former, or are the latter completely false if they claim to provide veridical knowledge of God? To my knowledge there is no completely convincing answer to the problem stated in this form. The most we can ever get is what in fact we mostly have—assertion and counter-assertion, according to premises which are nowhere stated. Now I am saying that there is no problem here; what I am after is a restatement of the problem in such a way as to lay bare the internal structure of the situation to which it relates.

Let me put it this way. Another description of the negative and positive poles of fulfilment is to say that the fulfilment stands in a relation of continuity and discontinuity to the prophecy which it fulfils. Within propositions s_{n-x} there are to be found elements which are organically continuous with others in propositions s_{a-m}. The real question which is being asked in the controversy over general and special revelation is whether there are any elements referred to in propositions s_{n-x} which are

continuous with any of the elements referred to in the propositions g_{a-m}. To give values to the symbols: given that there is
contained in Jesus Christ all that we shall ever require to know of
God, that in fact there we have to do with the fulness of God,
then is there some organic continuity between Him and not only
what we know of God from the Old Testament but also what
we know of God from the created order, or what we can anticipate
concerning God on the basis of the created order, or, more
generally still, from what we know of the created order?
When I state the problem in this way, at least three things
become clear to me of which I was not previously conscious.

(*a*) The very fact of the Incarnation implies continuity
between special Revelation and general revelation, and, more
widely still, the whole natural order. It is now customary to set
the Incarnation at a point in the thin red line of *Heilsgeschichte*—
the centre point, maybe—but the total significance of the
Incarnation is not comprehended unless we see converging
on that same point a line of secular history, the cosmos organised
out of relation to the known decrees and "mighty acts of God".
Until we see that other line, I cannot be sure that we have yet
shaken ourselves free of one of the earliest heresies of the faith,
namely, Docetism. Now it is not here intended that this
secular line is one purely of judgment, that it expresses the
wrath of God which reaches its culmination in the rejection of
Christ and the cry of dereliction. At this point it seems to me
Brunner is wrong when he finds in the world apart from Christ
only the wrathful God. The wrath of God is more unambiguously placarded in the Cross of Christ than it is over the
whole face of Nature. This line of secular history to which I
refer contains that same mixture of mercy and of judgment
which we associate with *Heilsgeschichte* but it differs from the
latter in that, whereas the latter is prophetic of the Divine
nature of the Incarnate Lord, it is prophetic of the human
nature.

(*b*) Looking at special Revelation prior to the Incarnation,
with that familiarity which breeds insensitivity, we grow to
think that there is an almost logical necessity governing the
relation of the propositions s_{a-m} and s_{n-x}. We forget that on the
one hand the men who knew most thoroughly the former were

totally unable to see how they were related to the latter, and that it was only when the Risen Christ spoke to the disciples that the scales fell from their eyes. Even here, there is no question but that all is *sola gratia*. If so, there seems to be no real difficulty in taking the further step of recognising that of the same grace the human nature which Our Lord took, the material order with which He made Himself one in being made flesh, was thereby affirmed to stand in continuity with special Revelation, for He was both human and Divine.

(*c*) What has not been sufficiently made clear in most of the ordinary discussions of the problem of special and general Revelation is that special Revelation itself has many things to say about general revelation. I am not thinking of a somewhat doubtful exegesis of the first two chapters of the Epistle to the Romans or of St. Paul on Mars Hill. Accepting the transcript of the problem as I have suggested above that we should, then we can call in the evidence of such a sentence as this: "The creation groaneth and travaileth waiting for the redemption of the Sons of God" (Rom. 8.22). The implication is that the natural order, which on the old reckoning was thought to be out of relation to special Revelation, is affirmed to be in organic continuity with it through the relation of expectation. If, too, all things consist of Christ, then it is no unwarranted leap to assume that their consistence prior to the coming of Christ is a foretaste by that fuller state into which they enter through the Incarnation. One feels that the Greek theologians could never have posed the problem of general and special Revelation; it was never a problem for the Logos Christology.

CHAPTER SEVEN

HISTORY AND THE INCARNATION

(b) THE INCARNATION AS REDEMPTIVE AND RECREATIVE

IN claiming that fulfilment is the original category for the description of the Incarnation, we must not fall into the error of suggesting that it is the only category. In fact, there is a real sense in which this category is formal: it does not indicate what it is that is fulfilled. To complete our treatment of the part which Incarnation plays in the construction of history, then it remains to supply content to the notion of fulfilment. At once it is clear that it is God's promise to save the world, God's purpose of salvation which is fulfilled in the Incarnation. The redemptive, recreative effect originated in history by the Incarnation may be observed in the following ways, each of which attempts to do justice to one of the great concepts in which the New Testament has sought to interpret the Incarnation and the Atonement, namely, (i) forgiveness, (ii) reconciliation, (iii) identification and (iv) victory.

(i) To begin with, we can easily see that the forgiveness achieved for man in the Life, Death and Resurrection of Our Lord is constitutive of history in so far as it has laid the basis for future possible renewals of personality which may come through the acceptance in faith by believers of the forgiveness that God constantly offers. It is quite amazing how even the most thoughtful of Christian people are duped into thinking that history is constituted of the follies and machinations of the rogues and ne'er-do-weels who catch the eye and the fancy of the roving reporters who staff our daily newspapers, and even of the activities of only slightly more important rogues who achieve a greater degree of permanence in our history textbooks; while all the time, day in and day out, countless thousands of honest Christian people are making life a richer and a sweeter thing for their fellows by deeds of consecration. I would reject outright any pretension that the quite fortuitous appearance of an action or event in newspaper or textbook, or

77

the failure of another event or action to achieve that kind of notoriety, could in itself prevent it from constituting the stuff of history, or on the contrary guarantee to it this function. If a Christian doctrine of history does no more than redress the balance of historical assessment in favour of honesty and decency as against perfidy and crime, then it has justified itself.

(ii) The redemptive, recreative effect of the Incarnation upon history is seen not only in its influence upon the lives and actions of redeemed people in the community but also in the changed status which the Incarnation gives it in the eyes of God. "God was in Christ reconciling the world unto Himself" is the Pauline account of this very fact, that whereas previously history was a thing alien to God, organised in open defiance of God, it is now through the Death of Christ at peace with God. Now admittedly the first-century mind did not mean by κόσμος what we mean by history, but undoubtedly the former will include the latter as the greater the less. If we accept the force of the word "reconcile"—and Biblical and Dogmatic theology has never been more inclined to do so in its whole history than it is today—then we have to face all the implications of such literality, and particularly this one, that the Death of Christ sets up a relation between God and the world that did not exist before. Another way of putting the matter is to say that history is now accepted by God and thirled by Him to His great purposes as it had never been before. Our generation does not have the difficulty which our predecessors had with the Biblical concept of the solidarity of man with man and of man with Nature: they, through their individualistic obsessions could envisage only conglomerations of units, or man against a background of Nature from which he felt himself cut off, and the Calvinistic doctrine of the *dominium* furthered the severance. So we find no difficulty in the idea that in the Atonement, not only are isolated individuals given a new status before God, but so also is the totality of history. By implication there are many new ways in which history may become related to God which were denied to it before.

(iii) But in accomplishing the salvation of the world, and in fact as the means by which He does so, God effects the identification of Himself with history. "He that knew no sin was made sin for us" (II Cor. 5.21). It was not some other history with which He identified Himself, some *Heilsgeschichte* without the sins and shortcomings and ambiguities of this kind of history that we know and help to make, but with this history in all its fallenness. This concept of identification is becoming, for me at least, the dominant one in the interpretation of the Atonement, and I should like to make these further comments upon it: (a) When this identification is accomplished in the Life, Death and Resurrection of Jesus Christ, there is no compromising of the Holiness and Righteousness of God through His identification with the fallenness of humanity and history. God does not cease to be holy. On the other hand, humanity and history, while they are redeemed through this identification, do not cease thereupon to evince some of the sinful qualities which they had before. They have not suddenly acquired the Divine Holiness, which is without spot or blemish. It is because this identification is of such a unique kind that many of the discussions of the sinlessness of Christ, arising from His assuming human nature, have a highly artificial character. They fail to relate the sinlessness to the vast process, beginning in the hidden places of the Godhead, of identification, and to realise that Christ's sinlessness is not an implicate of that identification so much as a way of describing it. (b) So we may add that holiness is identification, or involvement. The real sin of the Pharisees was contained in their name; they remained separate, cut off. Their religion was no bond between them and their fellow men; it hedged them about, so that their righteousness was self-righteousness, not primarily because they were conceited about it but because they kept it to themselves and it kept them to themselves. In Christ we see that holiness goes forth beyond itself, identifying itself with that which it would redeem, and at no point wondering whether its reputation is to be compromised thereby. Is He not the friend of publicans and sinners? The attitude of the Church to politics and society has, I feel sure, been largely dictated by a quite false notion of holiness, one which was in the last analysis Pharisaic. (c) It is the identification of God with history, involved in the Incarnation, which calls in question every suggestion that God steps into history and withdraws, having done His "mighty acts". There is a dangerous element of Deism involved in at least some of the interpretations of the now famous phrase *senkrecht von oben* which were certainly not intended by the originator of the phrase. Once the Incarnation has taken place there is no question of God stepping out of history, or of His contracting out of this once-for-all identification. To recur to a previous theme: the view that God does certain mighty acts in history both presupposes a wrong conception of history and mis-understands the consequences for history of the mightiest act of all.

(iv) Through the Incarnation, God in Christ puts the powers of darkness to final shame and through the victory of the Cross takes the moral ambiguity from history *as a whole*. To say so much is in fact to say two things. First, we are admitting that there has been moral ambiguity in history: it has not been ethically neutral, as if it were a colourless framework within which things happened. Next, we make the qualification that the moral ambiguity remains here and there throughout history, for the powers of darkness do not cease to be. What must be guarded against is any premature attempt to remove the ambiguity from the parts of history with all the assurance with which we claim it has been removed from the whole. In fact, the *Christus Victor* theme does not prove to be the easy principle of historical interpretation which it was thought to be, particularly in the later years of the War.

(c) THE INCARNATION AS CREATIVE

The previous characterisation of the Incarnation did justice to the way in which the Incarnation transforms the history of man from something which merits the condemnation of God into a thing acceptable. Now we draw attention to the new possibilities which the Incarnation introduces into history. It does so in three ways:

(i) The first follows immediately from what has been said about redemption. The basis of forgiveness secured in Jesus Christ introduces new possibilities of moral character and moral action which were impossible under the pre-Christian religion and ethic. When we think of religion in history our minds run almost automatically to the wars, the persecutions and disagreements, ignoring the saints and heroes who have in every generation witnessed to the power of the Risen Christ, through whom they were more than conquerors. It may be that there is not so much to say about them as there is about the others; as Professor A. E. Taylor once remarked, "Bad men often make more interesting material for ethical study than good men, concerning whom we can sometimes know no more than that they are good." The bad characters in fiction, drama and poetry have always had a reputation for stealing the admiration, if not also sometimes even the affections of the readers. So in a curious way in history goodness is almost an actual disqualification for fame; and yet the wealth of value imparted to history through the presence in it of good people is quite imponderable.

(ii) The Incarnation is creative of a second group of possibilities in history in so far as through the Creation of the Church God has a new sphere of operation within history. Without committing ourselves to any specific interpretation of a phrase which I feel sure St. Paul never intended to be the subject of controversy which it has become, and without any excuse for using the phrase without a lexicon of qualifications, we may say that through the Church, which is the Body of Christ, God exerts an influence over a range in history incommensurate with anything that existed before, even in the Old Israel. This range is not to be simply measured in tidy judgments about the strength of the Church in the world-order, or by the numerical membership of the Church, or even by the truthfulness of the Church's proclamation to the witness of the Apostles. The presence of God in His Church may be a mystery, part of the great mystery of the Incarnation, but it is nevertheless a real presence; since He is present in His Church He is thereby present in history.

(iii) What must also be said is that the Incarnation is creative not only of a whole host of higher moral achievements and of new ways in which God may work His will in history, but also of a whole new *range* of moral possibilities of evil as well as of good. In fact, the introduction of the one implies the other necessarily. *Corruptio optimi pessimum.* Since the corruption of the best is always an open possibility where you have human nature in action, the worst is therefore always a historical possibility. The tragedy of human history after the Incarnation is that that possibility is so often converted to reality. The apocalyptic chapters towards the end of St. Matthew's Gospel are not so far removed from the kind of history which we know, and they do not really require to be touched by the philosopher's stone of demythologisation to be translated into our kind of world and our kind of language. The introduction of the Christ into history is bound to elicit from history something very like the anti-Christ, creating, as it were, a completely new dimension of moral possibility, in both depth and height hitherto undreamt of. At this point it becomes clear how difficult it is to give any simple and unqualified answer to the problem of the influence of Christianity upon history, or for that matter upon, say, Western civilisation. The idealists and the moralists have tended to estimate this influence in only one direction, the positive, whereas a more realistic—and truthful—account would have to recognise the negative and evil influence exerted. If one may speak in this way, the history of what we call Western civilisation, if it is a good deal better than it would have been without Christianity, is also a very great deal worse.

(d) THE INCARNATION AS PROSPECTIVE

As Barth has said, history as we now know it is "between the times", between the time of the First Coming of Our Lord and that Second Coming, the *Parousia*, as the New Testament calls it, when that same Lord will stand revealed and history and the world-order as we know them will pass away. This history between the times is therefore both forward-looking and backward-looking. So far in our exposition we have been dealing mainly with the latter, in our discussions of the ways in which the past promises have been fulfilled in the present, and how the sins of the past have been blotted out in the Death of Christ. In order, then, to see just how the Incarnation as prospective constitutes the kind of history which we affirm in the Christian doctrine, it will be necessary to comment upon the ways in which the First Coming of Christ is related to the Second Coming.

(i) It can not be repeated too frequently that the Christ who shall appear at the *Parousia* is that same Christ who has already sojourned among men. This must be said because the attempt is so often made to discredit the Doctrine of the Second Coming on the ground that the Christ who is to come is the Judge, not the strong lover of men with whom we meet in the Gospels. The real answer to this kind of complaint is to say that the First Coming of Christ into the world was as much the judgment of the world as the Second. "He came to convict the world of sin and righteousness and judgment." The sin of man was as truly condemned and judged as it was forgiven at Calvary. Christ is Judge in both Comings as He is Saviour. What should be added, however, is that the Second Coming is not a Revelation in the sense in which we have come so to describe the First. It is rather interesting that the New Testament used the term "reveal" for that final appearance, and that actually that is the normal New Testament connotation of the term. He does not come then to reveal hidden mysteries of the Godhead but to execute before our eyes and in no symbol that which we already know will be.

(ii) The Second Coming is in several respects the completion of what Christ had already initiated in the First Coming. To begin with, we can reaffirm what we have just been saying, that the judgment of the world is completed in this Second Coming and that God's time of waiting comes to an end. The powers of evil and darkness, while they lost the decisive battle to *Christus Victor* on Calvary and in the Resurrection, have continued the struggle. At the *Parousia*, the struggle ends. It is, too, God's intimation that the Gospel offer is not open indefinitely; man has to close with it decisively or the offer is withdrawn.

(iii) It is therefore possible for us to say that there are in fact two relations existing between the affirmation of the First Coming and that of the Second. On the one hand, it is clear that they both stand side by side in Holy Scripture and that accordingly we affirm both with equal authority. The relation between the two doctrines would be external and very much that which holds between any two doctrines of the faith, thus, that between the doctrine of Creation and that of the Fall. On the other hand, it is possible to draw a more intimate relation between the two, and to say that the First Coming implies the Second Coming. This assertion is really not nearly as simple as it looks. For example, there is a submerged premise involved in it, a premise which takes into account the ways in which the world as we know it seems not to stultify, but to place in question, certain of the things that we hold to be implied by the First Coming. Of the First Coming we say that it was the means by which God in Christ conquered sin: yet men continue to sin. God in Christ has the victory over the rulers of this present evil age, yet they continue to exist. So if the Scriptures had not affirmed a Second Coming, then it appears that we should have required to postulate one, if for no other reason, to safeguard the truths established by the First Coming. When the latter kind of construction has been put on the relation of the two doctrines by those who were particularly keen to maintain the Second Coming—as a great many people have been doing since the Evanston discussions on "the hope of the world"—then, in fact, a disservice has been done to the doctrine for two reasons. First, a very clear impression is given that the Second Coming is intended to make up for deficiencies left in the wake of the First Coming, as if the latter were not in itself complete. Secondly, the way has been opened up for those who, claiming that there is no genuine logical implication of the Second Coming by the First, argue that the Doctrine of the Second Coming is a psychological compensation for the miseries of this world, and that its emergence in the Primitive Church is due to the early persecutions. Others see the same reason for its re-emergence in Germany immediately after each of the two World Wars. Yet the alternative is not to revert to the first position and to say that there is only the loosest external connection between the First and the Second Coming. The real answer to the problem is to affirm that it is improper to regard the First and the Second Coming of Christ as if they were two separate sets of events, and to regard them as parts of the one single great fact of Christ. This is indeed what the second article of the Apostles' Creed intends when it classes the clause concerning the Second Coming—"from whence He shall come to judge the quick and the dead"—along with all the other things that it has to say about Him in the previous clauses, as if it were quite co-ordinate with them. In saying the Creed we affirm our belief in a Christ who did *a b c* and *d*, and not in a Christ who did *a b* and *c*, and who in addition did, or rather, will do, *d*. Christological expositions have not greatly helped in this connection, because they have presented the Second Coming as if it were a doctrine additional to that of the Incarnation, and not an integral, essential part of it.

In the light, then, of the relation in which the First Coming stands to the Second Coming, we may go on to describe the ways in which the Incarnation as prospective determines the character which history has "between the times". (i) If history "between the times" for the Christian is prospective, it is not so in precisely the same way as it was for the Jew who had not received the fulfilment of the promises. For that reason it must be finally unscholarly and even unchristian to find the clue to the Apocalyptic passages in the Gospels in the extra-canonical or pre-Christian literature, however similar they are superficially. The return of Him who has come is something very different from the Coming of the Messiah for the first time, and accordingly the basic attitudes of those who wait must differ, and so too the signs of the end. In other words, the character of Christ has imposed a quality upon authentic Christian Apocalyptic which is missing from the non-Christian. There is, for example, the *conviction* that Christ will come in all His glory for *He* has said He will come; there is the awareness that it is no shadowy unknown person who will come but One who has already walked and talked with His own; there is assurance as to the *nature* of that Coming; and so on. These things are absent from the non-Christian Apocalyptic, while their presence in the Christian is our only justification for retaining it as so primitive a part of the *kerugma*. Antiquity of documentation in this case would have been a poor justification for its retention if the mind of Our Lord had not been indelibly impressed upon it.

(ii) The Christian living and acting in the history "between the times" knows that he has already laid hands upon the end things. He has already entered the *eschaton*. This is the truth contained in the phrase "realised eschatology", and it has become customary to illustrate the idea in several ways, some of which we have already anticipated. The Christian now shares in the final victory of Christ over sin and death. In every celebration of the Sacrament of the Lord's Supper he shares proleptically in the Marriage Feast of the Lamb. His participation in the Communion of Saints is something more than just a taste of the fulness that is yet to be: he is now one with all the redeemed in earth and heaven. Kierkegaard used the phrase "contemporary disciple" to draw attention to the fact that regardless of the age in which we live we are all as contemporary with Jesus Christ as Peter, James and John. We would perhaps say that through the Holy Spirit and within the fellowship of the Church, when the Word of God is read and proclaimed, when the faithful join in prayer and praise, then Christ is heard and His will made known unto mercy and judgment. But if realised eschatology be the truth, then we must also be said to be contemporary with the *eschaton*, not merely in some vague metaphorical way, but in a quite literal way. It is in this connection that I think we may legitimately talk about different "times", but I would be very careful to emphasise that this "time" within which we stand contemporaneous with the First Coming on the one hand and with the Second Coming on the other, is not a substitute for the other time in which we live and which is the structure for our daily lives. In fact it completely presupposes it: for without this ordinary time it would be impossible for us to speak about the "then" of the First Coming, the "now" of the present, and that other "then" that is yet to be.

(iii) It is usual to interpret realised escahatology in terms chiefly of the apprehension by the believer now of the *good* things of the *eschaton*. But since the *Parousia* is strongly associated with judgment, a sterner note must also be present. To reject here and now the offer of God in Christ, to turn aside from the challenge when He meets us, this may in fact prove to be the anticipation of the Last Judgment. It is this proleptically present word and act of judgment which is the ground of the urgency that must be a characteristic of every genuine proclamation of the Word of God. It is the knowledge of this fact which must drive us to our knees at some time during our sermon preparation, lest having preached the Gospel we should ourselves be cast away, or being entrusted with the Gospel we fail to convey it unequivocally. In saying that the Last Judgment is projected forward to take its place within history, I do not mean what some of our predecessors intended when they said that the judgment that takes place when a man rejects the Gospel now is *all* that there is to the Last Judgment. It is only a part of what is meant, but it is a part, which is more than some of the post-Evanston apocalyptists would allow.

(iv) It is not always realised how great a tension this position between the times creates for the Christian in history. In his private ethical life he stands between the redemption achieved once for all and that consummation of all moral striving in the end-time, as a sinner who has within his members a principle that wars against the Spirit, a sinner redeemed and yet being redeemed. In his judgments upon contemporary history he sees it now as the field in which *Christus Victor* is working out His victory, and again he sees "not yet all things put under Him"; and from these not simply compatible interpretations, it is difficult to draw unambiguous conclusions. So too, when the question of his own participation in history arises, he is at times torn between the inactivity bred of the conviction that the issues have all been settled and the fear that crisis ($\kappa\rho\acute{\iota}\sigma\iota\varsigma$) is about to overtake him, and that his next decision may have an eternal significance for him. Any truly Christian doctrine of history must admit the influence that this tension introduces into history and must dissociate itself from the idealistic interpretations, allegedly Christian, which would claim to rationalise the whole course of history. On the other hand, when we observe that the Church has not played a completely intelligible part in the affairs of men in the last two thousand years, then it may be wise to remind ourselves that this is not attributable solely to the shameful weakness and folly of the Church but perhaps rather to the inherent nature of Christianity. In fact, given the curious status of the Christian Church between the times, the sort of history which we have is very much what one might expect. For my own part I prefer saying this to assuming an almost intolerable burden of guilt for what has been often regarded as the ineffectiveness of the Church in the world. We have enough guilt to bear without contracting an extra amount to which we bear no direct relation. If we really believe that Christ bore the sin and guilt of the world, then it is almost morbid for us to go out of our way to amass some specially for ourselves; yet this is just the kind of morbidity which discussions with Marxists breed in us. It is not asserted, of course, that the Church is completely blameless in history or that it has never been in error or callous or cruel; but only that there exists an affected penitence over the social, economic and political sins of the Church, which is offensive in that it is directed more to the Kremlin than to the throne of grace.

(v) One of the main questions to arise in the examination of the prospective effects which the category of the Incarnation introduces into history is that of whether we can legitimately go on to affirm teleology in the Christian doctrine of history. Clearly we can not do so if by teleology we mean a view which postulates an innate purpose in history working itself out. History does not have a *telos* towards which it is relentlessly moving, a *telos* which, from within, determines what happens in history. Exponents of one type of progress theory used to affirm that there was an evolutionary principle at work in history directing it towards a *telos* of perfection. Even some pessimistic interpreters of history who see it as the tale of man's defiance of God come little short of regarding sin as a similar *telos* in history. The Christian affirmation that the prospective quality of history derives from the Second Coming is the virtual denial of all immanent teleology native to history, but it leaves open the possibility that a teleology may be introduced *ab extero*. This position could be arrived at by an extension of our previous discussion of realised eschatology. If we take the letter E as the symbol of the *eschaton*, and e_1, e_2, e_3, . . . as the events in history which anticipate the *eschaton*, events in which it is proleptically realised, then we may say that in virtue of this relation in which e_1, e_2, e_3, . . . stand to E, they also stand in some relation to one another, e_1, . . . e_2, . . . e_3, and so on.   In other words there is in history a *telos* which is being worked out and which is a projection in time of the *eschaton* which stands at the end or at the edge of time.   To say so much is not to affirm that this teleological series is perfectly discernible even by the eye of faith ; if the series is constituted by the relation of each of the members to E, then we can not expect either to affirm or to discover that kind of continuity. On the other hand, because each of the members is related to E by the relation of proleptic realisation, then it would be strange if they did not stand in some relation to one another.   When we translate what we have been saying back into literal language it can be easily seen to be true, for the kind of teleology which the Christian living between the times experiences, is just that which we have indicated—it does not form a completely continuous series, at least from our vantage point, but several events do from time to time link up to form a continuous series; while all along he affirms that the rationale of the entire series is to be found in the *eschaton*, and that since this *eschaton* is one, it must inevitably impart some intrinsic unity to the series.

(vi) The actual concept of the *eschaton* occupies a larger place in contemporary theology than it did in the thinking even of the Primitive Church.   In fact I would be prepared to say that the *eschaton* as we use the term was scarcely present to the minds of the early Christians.   The term *Parousia* constituted the content of the End for them, but not that rather impersonal thing which we so often mean by that term.   It was the παρουσία χριστοῦ, so that the subject of their thought was the ἔσχατος, a Person whom they had known and loved, instead of an event.   While it is still necessary to remind ourselves that this personal element must be constantly before our minds in the interpretation of the End, nevertheless it is not implied that we ought to cease to speak of the event which is the *eschaton*.   We may still use the term, doing so, as it were, with our eyes open.   In contemporary usage, then, the idea of the *eschaton* has two elements.   First, it means completely accomplished *telos*, the fulfilment of the mighty purposes which

God advanced so far in the Incarnation of Our Lord. Secondly, it means *finis*, the end in the ordinary sense that there is just no more to come. It is the presence in the notion of this double element which is the explanation of its apparent versatility. Because it is *telos* it may be projected forward into the events in the teleological series previously described which anticipate it. Because it is *finis* it does not hereby lose its position as the end-term in the series. Because it is the consummation of the *series* it is continuous with the proleptic realisations of itself, and, as the Gospels indicate, takes place within this world and the history that we know. Because it is the *consummation* of the series it is discontinuous with the earlier events as embodying something which was absent from them.

The foregoing will provide us with the answer to two comments that have been made in recent times on the notion of the *eschaton*. It has been pointed out recently that it is improper for exponents of the notion of realised eschatology to speak of an *eschaton* which turned out to be a long way off the true *eschaton*. If an *eschaton* is not last it is no *eschaton*. Quite clearly while such a view has etymology on its side it does not appreciate the complexity of the idea it is discussing. *Eschaton*, as we have shown, is not simply *finis*. To say that it is, is to identify history with the time process. The second comment goes in the opposite direction, and affirms virtually that *eschaton* is unrelated to *finis*. On this view the *telos* of history is already fulfilled in the Advent of Our Lord, and consequently the *eschaton* is already here. It is even supported by the affirmation that were the historical process to cease at any moment after the First Coming, then history would have been as complete and as completed as otherwise. Such a position is untenable for the following reasons. To begin with, it rather makes nonsense of history since the Incarnation, reducing it to the status of shadow-play. I am not sure but that it almost nullifies the Incarnation, which surely affirms the importance of the history consequent to itself as the field within which is brought home to the hearts of sinful men the whole significance of what God had done in Jesus Christ. It also fails to do justice to the fact that God is working out His purpose in the time between the times, and that this time

is no more expendable than any other period in which He wills
to act. Further it does not quite appreciate the way in which
the elements in the *eschaton* as delineated above are related to
one another. The *finis*, the time end to history, is an outward
symbol of the accomplishment of the *telos*; it is unthinkable
that one should occur without the other. Any suggestion
then that *finis* could occur without the fulfilment of the *telos*
makes the relation of the two to one another purely external
and fortuitous, and introduces an element of pure chance into
history at the point where God's purposes could be most
completely stultified, namely, the eve of their fulfilment.

(e) THE INCARNATION AS INTEGRATIVE

Finally, and on the basis of the previous characterisations
of the function of the Incarnation in relation to history, we may
say that this category is *integrative*. It introduces a unity
which we could not ascribe to history even by the use of the
category of Providence. We have already seen how, in part at
least, the category of Incarnation integrates history, in that it is
fulfilment, but I want particularly to draw attention to the
following rather different aspects of this particular characteristic
of Incarnation:

(i) First of all, it has a retroactive effect upon past history,
so that in a way the Incarnation could be said to alter the
character of events once they are past. On the one hand, it
does so by virtue of the very fact that it is fulfilment. Given
a series $a\ b\ c\ d$ at time t_1, at which time the members of the
series are problematic in character, many things may be said
about them but the full significance of them cannot be grasped.
Now at time t_2 appears event X, which stands to $a\ b\ c\ d$ in the
relation to them which we describe as fulfilment (f). What I
am maintaining is that the fact that $a\ b\ c\ d$ are, subsequently to
their happening, found to be related to X by f actually alters
their character. In this new relation in which they stand at
time t_2 and in which they did not stand at time t_1 because X
had not then happened, they acquire attributes that they
did not have before. I do not just mean that we who live at
time t_3 are now able to understand them better than men who

lived between t_1 and t_2, or that we can have a view of them now which was impossible then, and that the difference is something subjective to the observers; I really do mean that there can take place qualitative changes in events after they have happened, or more accurately, that the Incarnation effects this kind of change, for I am not at present concerned with the question of whether it happens in any other connections. On the other hand, we reach the same result if we think in terms of the forgiveness which results from the Death of Christ. Prior to the Atonement, human history was under the judgment of God, a judgment all the more complete for all the evidences that Israel, for example, had had of Divine mercy. When God in Jesus Christ reconciled the world to Himself, He not only set individual men in a new relation to Himself, He did so also with human history. In other words He actually altered the character of events that had already taken place. This demonstration is not simply one in elementary logic, for upon its validity depends our whole contention that the Incarnation is constitutive of history, and that it is integrative of history. Short of some such demonstration we should have to be content with the much less inclusive statements that the Incarnation gives us a point of view from which to interpret history but that it does nothing actually to history itself.

(ii) But the integrative effect of the Incarnation must be traced also in relation to those events which have happened since Christ, and which also seem to be out of relation to the Church in which Christ is so really present in the world and not to be immediately relatable to Revelation. To these events, as to those which happened before Christ, the Incarnation stands in the same relations of fulfilment and negation. I am thinking particularly of social systems, of moral codes and orders of justice, and of the struggles in which men involve themselves for the maintenance of these, or to the altering of them for others that they hold before themselves as ideals. There is a sense, too, in which all history subsequent to Christ stands under the judgment of God and in this relation has characteristics that it would not otherwise have. The Life, Death and Resurrection of Jesus Christ were, as Aulèn rightly points out, God's own victory over the powers of evil and darkness in the world; and if that victory was real, then in human affairs a limit is set beyond which sin and evil cannot go. These limits set up real relations within history, and are not for the Christian fictitious principles of interpretation: once he allows them to become so he has departed from the Christian analysis of history. But the suffering and the misery that are in the world are not, on such an analysis, left out of consideration. It is to me significant that both Professor Niebuhr and Professor Butterfield should emphasise the fact that in the Cross God took to Himself the problem of human suffering and sin, and therefore identified Himself with them, or, as Professor Butterfield says, took the problem into Himself. If these sentences mean what they say, and I feel that they do, for they take us so very close to the heart of the Christian Gospel, then it follows that by the Incarnation an actual and not just a potential relationship is set up between God and those of His creatures who are suffering or are in any kind of distress. And that kind of connection is what I am maintaining makes history what it is for the Christian.

CHAPTER EIGHT

HISTORY AND FREEDOM

IT will by this time be apparent that the Christian doctrine of history does not regard freedom as the sole category constitutive of history. It is not always as clearly appreciated how extensively circumscribed the category of freedom is. In fact, in the now outmoded controversy over freedom and necessity, both sides began from a common premise which prevented either of them from ultimately refuting the other, namely, that these two views on the inner nature of human activity were mutually exclusive, and that therefore between them they exhausted the field. The result was that they both had to overstate their cases in order to have any case. The libertarian gave the impression that the human agent approached any situation calling for action with a mind free from all prejudices and predilections, and that his decision to act in a specific way came like a bolt from the blue, unpredictably and spontaneously. In this way all relation between character and action was denied and the improvement of character rendered quite impossible. Indeed, it would be impossible even to postulate character under these circumstances, except as a series of unrelated actions. The determinist, on the other hand, regards the analysis of human behaviour rather as a problem in dynamics, as the definition of the various parallelograms of forces out of which the behaviour has originated. So completely is the field plotted that there is no possibility of spontaneous, undetermined action at all. This controversy over free will and necessity lasted as long as it did not so much through the conviction which each conveyed as to the soundness of its arguments in its own favour, as through the effectiveness with which each was able to demonstrate the inconclusiveness of the opponent's arguments. At the very outset, then, I am here refusing to be drawn into the old controversy, contending that freedom occurs within a certain structure, the ingredients in which may be fairly definitely indicated. They are necessity (as variously characterised above, Chapter 3), grace and selfhood. It is the juxtaposition in which freedom is set in relation to these three entities which is the clue to the very important but at the same time extremely complex part which freedom plays in the constitution of history.

(i) *Freedom and Necessity.* We have already said something about the way in which freedom operates within the structure of necessity—in the case of the person in a political crisis, who finds that certain lines of action are quite beyond the reach of possibility because his predecessors in office have acted as they did, under the inhibiting influence of geography, socio-economic conditioning, as well as of the "history that works over our heads". For our present purpose we may add that Divine Sovereignty prescribes that certain excesses of human behaviour lead to certain results which no will however free can ever change or deny, results as clearly seen by non-Christian interpreters as by Christians, and empirically observable even amid all the moral obscurities which make history so difficult to interpret. "God is not mocked" is an assertion which is as true of universal history as it is of our own personal relations to God. The question which at this point becomes inescapable is: if the structure of necessity is so omnipresent, upon what grounds is freedom affirmed? The answer to this question is twofold.

On the one hand, the most obvious body of evidence for freedom is the almost universal fact of moral responsibility. It is no novelty in this field to draw attention to the findings of the anthropologists, who are fairly unanimous in their judgment that no matter how primitive the code of the community, there is almost invariably a sense of responsibility felt by the members towards it. What is more of a novelty is the way in which those who are committed to some form of metaphysical determinism, of theoretical a-morality, unwittingly confess to an attenuated sense of moral responsibility. You have, for example, the moral indignation of the Marxist over the exploitation of the proletariat by the bourgeoisie, who are held to be morally responsible for the sufferings which the former have undergone, and shall be punished accordingly. Yet moral responsibility implies freedom to have done otherwise, or, at least, to have entertained the possibility of doing otherwise. Those who, as in some forms of existentialism, make a parade of their rejection of accepted moral codes, come very near to making an obligation of their rejection; and indeed within the social group conform with the appropriate sense of duty done, experienced by the most backward member of a primitive tribe. Brunner (*The Divine Imperative*) seems to be sound in following Kant in this affirmation of the co-implication of moral responsibility and freedom; even though he may not be so sound in his further contention that this sense of moral responsibility implies another type of responsibility, namely, answerability to the address of the living God. It is therefore of great interest that Orthodox and Neo-Orthodox theology has endeavoured to retain the reality of moral responsibility, even at the point of denying that human freedom persisted after the Fall. A necessity operating from within rather than from without, as in most of the forms of the category of necessity which we have considered, destroys the freedom which is generally regarded as the pre-condition of moral behaviour. It is not a way out of this problem to say that the freedom that is lost is freedom towards God, whereas man still retains his freedom towards man and Nature; for man's unfreedom towards God will reveal itself nowhere more clearly than in his unfreedom in the two other spheres. Nor is it more satisfactory to say that while a necessity constrains man to sin, he is free to choose the forms of his sin; because, on any serious view of sin, it is likely that the sin which constrains the man to turn aside from the good to prefer the evil will also constrain him to choose the greater evil in preference to the lesser, disguising the true situation with the rationalisation that the lesser is really the greater.

On the other hand, I am convinced then that we cannot find an adequate ground for the affirmation of freedom within the structure of the different forms of the category of necessity so long as we remain within the confines of Kantian ethics. It is significant that Kant had to pass beyond these confines himself, even to solve the problems which his ethics raised. The ultimate Christian ground for the affirmation of freedom is the offer of redemption made by God to man through the

Gospel of Jesus Christ. The genuineness of this offer implies the reality of the freedom in which it is either accepted or rejected. This is said in full recognition of the fact that the acceptance of the offer is made only through the grace of God. For whatever grace is, and whatever it does, it does not replace the human will with some higher will, or substitute the freedom of God for the freedom of man. God's will is that man should freely embrace the offer He makes, so that the very depths of his being may participate in it. For the Christian, the freedom of man is postulated in the Gospel, and is not an inductive inference from the researches of the anthropologists—in other words, is not an immediately observable fact. Such an admission is in no way unique to the Christian interpretation of freedom ; it is involved in the libertarian's, as well as in that which sees freedom as self-determination.

(ii) *Freedom and Grace.* In our affirmation of the way in which the Gospel offer presupposes human freedom we have had occasion to refer to grace. For the purposes of the present discussion, we may say that grace is a condition of the possibility of freedom and of the expression of freedom. It is so particularly at two points. First, if the Gospel offer may be appropriated only in freedom, it is of grace that that freedom operates. While therefore it is usual at this stage to speak of the paradox of grace, it is to be remembered that the two members of the paradox are not co-ordinate; the one conditions the other's existence and in addition limits the form which it may take, reducing the possibilities until there remains only the possibility of freedom unto faith. What is not always recognised in this same connection is that the situation may be construed in another way to show that freedom supplies content to grace. The position towards which we might seem to be moving is that either we must discover a new conception of paradox or hold that the grace-freedom situation is not properly describable as a paradox. The customary interpretation of paradox is that it involves the affirmation of *A* and *Not-A* in respect of the same entities and in the same reference. *A* and *Not-A* are assumed to be logical contradictories and not simply contraries, and between them to exhaust the field. Perhaps Kant's Antinomies are the clearest example of what is meant. In any case, A and $Not\text{-}A$ are logically co-ordinate. This is just what is not the case with freedom and grace. The one conditions the other, for it is grace that creates the possibility of freedom. Further, there is no common field which grace and freedom between them exhaust, as if grace were responsible for certain of the actions of men, while freedom is responsible for the remainder. Secondly, in addition to conditioning the possibility of freedom, grace,—as it were, at another level—limits the range of the actions in which freedom may possibly express itself. This very matter was the subject of controversy between St. Paul and the members of some of the Churches which he had founded; they thought that grace created an unlimited range of moral—and immoral—activity. St. Paul's description of the fruits of the Spirit is his reminder that there are some things that are impossible for the morally free. So, too, in another connection, he has to say that the utterance that Jesus Christ is not the Lord is not a true utterance in the Spirit. Grace, then, together with the morality which is one of its expressions, is not the least important part of that structure within which freedom operates.

(iii) *Freedom and the Self.* Freedom is limited from within by the very nature of selfhood. The self I should regard as a complex of mental states and processes, related to a human body in a way in which it is related to no other piece of matter and in which no other piece of matter is related to it. The self that is, is, as the late Professor G. F. Stout maintained, an embodied self. Human volitions, therefore, are not to be regarded as mental occurrences which happen haphazardly within the mental stream; they form part of the complex self and issue from what we might call the dominant motive-pattern of the self. When we speak then of the freedom of the will we are not saying that the will is absolutely unmotivated. In fact, in view of the nature of the self we must add that the range of choices lying before the self is limited because of motive-patterns set up within the self by its previous choices. In a way freedom of the will must be spoken of in terms of self-determination, but even such determination is not complete, for not infrequently we commit actions that are contrary to dominant motive-patterns and besides no one of us is so completely integrated a personality that his behaviour can with any degree of accuracy be correlated with unified motive-structures. In any case, there occurs in every human action something that cannot be resolved without remainder into its antecedents, in every act of will something completely novel which is not the dynamic resultant of two sides of a psychological parallelogram of forces. This was what St. Augustine had in mind when he said that there is no efficient cause of the will.

I am here more particularly interested in the two most significant expressions of freedom—most significant, that is, for the Christian analysis of history—sin and faith.

(a) You will recall that in our discussion of the category of necessity we examined what Butterfield calls the "gravitational pull" in all history, the tendency to self-interest, to which witness is borne by sociologists, psychologists and moral philosophers, none of whom were at this point influenced by any particularly religious presuppositions. While it was essential there to draw attention to the necessary quality of the "gravitational pull", and while, too, it could be dealt with in a purely secular way, the whole truth about the situation is much more complex. On the one hand, while there is a "gravitational pull" in the direction of self-interest, that "pull" is not completely determinant of human behaviour; the fallacy in Kant's moral psychology lay in his saying that it was. I think that there is certain genius in Butterfield's choice of the word "pull", which suggests that while there may be a natural tendency in that direction, other forces, such as Divine grace, may operate to produce a tendency in another direction. In addition, as we have just indicated, the fact that even in those actions where we act most in our own interest, we are nevertheless prepared to acknowledge responsibility and therefore its correlate, freedom, rather indicates that the "pull" was not all-determining. On the other hand, it is necessary to give a Christian account of those elements in human nature which so catastrophically disrupt human history and produce the results which H. A. L. Fisher describes so pessimistically. These elements may variously be said to be defiance of God, man's contradiction of both his origin and his destiny, his failure to love his brother as himself or as one of the brethren for whom Christ died, his *hybris*, his setting himself up in the place which rightfully belongs to God, and his arrogating to himself attributes which belong properly only to God, and so on. The comprehensive term for all these expressions of human freedom is, of course, *sin*, which in accordance with at least one of the many insights of the Biblical story of the Fall must be regarded as the abuse of freedom. So radical, so universal is this abuse of freedom that some form of Doctrine of Original Sin seems to me to be inescapable, some form which does full justice to the fact that fallen human nature, for all its inherent depravity, still sins responsibly, and which sees in every sinful human action just that freedom for defiance of God which is classically expressed in Adam's sin against God. For whatever we say about the "gravitational pull", the proper place for sin is within the category of freedom.

(*b*) *Faith*. The second expression of freedom with which we are most particularly concerned here is that of faith, which I should regard as the free response of sinful creatures to the bounty of the Creator, to the love of the Redeemer and to the comfort of the Holy Spirit, a response which issues in a life which endeavours to do God's will, in a heart which seeks to love Him and in a mind which quests after the truth which He Himself is. While therefore the Christian, for purposes of ordinary discussion, has to employ descriptions of freedom which are drawn from what we might call lower dimensions, at the level of faith he finds himself, alongside St. Augustine, saying that it is only in faith in, and love towards, God that man is truly free; and with St. Paul that freedom in sin is in fact bondage. It is then no exaggeration to say that it is only in that expression of freedom which is faith that man properly appreciates that other expression of freedom which is sin for what it truly is. It is in this kind of context that we must understand St. Paul's words that "what is not of faith is sin", the implication being that wherever man's life is not oriented to God in a response of heart and mind and will to God's bounty and love and comfort, there it is lived in sin.

But there is a still deeper truth which the Christian Church has never failed to emphasise, in spite of the disrupting effects of such an emphasis upon the tidiness of the little systems that we try to set up. This truth is that even man's response in faith to God takes place through the indwelling of God, an indwelling which is alternatively described in terms of the paradox of grace, or in those of the immanence of the Holy Spirit. The former has now become associated with the name of Professor D. M. Baillie (*God was in Christ*), while the latter has been forcefully stated by Karl Barth, who speaks of God from below meeting God from above. Now we have already seen, in discussing Providence, that God's Revelation of Himself is not uniform in history, that some at least of the "fragmentariness" of history is due to this fact, and, in examining the implications of the Incarnation for the analysis of history, that there was a special Revelation completely specified as to time and space. But I have not so far, and purposely, introduced the term *kairos*. For it is not until there is a response in faith of the human being to the Revelation of God, either in Providence and under the Old Testament dispensation, or in the Person and Work of Jesus Christ, that these situations can be called *kairoi*. For it is the whole situation—Revelation and response in faith—that constitutes the *kairos*. The importance of the concept for us in this present analysis is that these *kairoi* happen, you might say, at the heart of historical process, to persons and societies who are engaged in historical activities. As Professor N. W. Porteous has pointed out, it is not satisfactory in describing the Christian view of history, to speak only as if this amounted to the recital of "the mighty acts of God", for these acts of God always occurred within a specific setting, and evoked a definite response in faith of the believers who, by God's grace, comprehended what God was doing in these mighty acts. It is therefore a false abstraction to treat the mighty acts in isolation either from their historical setting or from the response of faith.

It is necessary at this stage to indicate the implications that follow from this close relating of sin and faith to the category of freedom, which like all the other categories is, on this present analysis, taken to be constitutive of history, and not only as vehicles of its interpretation. What, in effect, we are here saying is that belief and unbelief (or sin) are not two standpoints which those who have these attitudes to the content of the Christian Gospel can take up, as it were, outside of history, two external positions from which they may gaze synoptically over the vast stretches of the human endeavour, assessing its meanings, and describing its various patterns, like visitors from another planet. Nor are they two ways of interpreting a body of "facts" that are objectively the same for both of them. On the contrary, as expressions of the category of freedom, they are themselves actually constitutive of history. The unbelief which a person A B chooses to have in relation to the work of God in Christ, or his sinful rejection of God's offer of succour and grace, or his willing refusal to relate the mighty acts of God meaningfully or existentially to his life or to his view of the world and of history, that unbelief, when it is taken along with the other categories that we should regard as operating at that time, is constitutive of history of his time. So *mutatis mutandis* is the faith of someone who trusts in God. Let us put the same position in a more extreme form, which is nevertheless not an exaggeration: a subjective attitude, an interpretation however private and subjective to the person who holds it, is an objective occurrence, a historical event. It is this involvement of the individual human being in the actual constituting of history through the category of freedom which, in my judgment, makes it well-nigh impossible for him to extricate himself from it to create for himself an island of subjectivity. For even his subjectivity is part of the process from which he is endeavouring to extricate himself.

HISTORY AND MEMORY

Obviously, the relation of memory to history is most important for any understanding of the latter, and consequently a good deal has been made of the subject in recent years; but the greatest care has to be taken, otherwise a certain amount of confusion will creep into our analysis. Some writers have almost elevated memory into being the only category of history, or at least have assigned to it a place of supreme importance. For example, we have the statement variously made by Dilthey,

Berdyaev and Rust that "history is the remembered past", or simply that "history is memory". Here we have a fallacy of over-simplification. The equation suggested cannot be made, for the following reasons:

(i) As Collingwood has so clearly maintained, a great deal of the energy of historians is devoted to the task of discovering events, facts or material which no one has remembered, and in relation to which there is no extant direct evidence. Of course, for this type of reconstruction of events for which there is no remembered evidence, the historian must have some basis in what has been remembered; but the actual reconstruction is made by means of elaborate processes of inference, assisted to no little extent by the imagination of the historian. Once his account of the newly established facts has been accepted by the other competent scholars in the field, then the fact that this account rests upon no basis in recorded memory is not held to make it any less historical than accounts of other events which do have that kind of basis.

(ii) But, in addition, the position of events which have a basis in memory is not accepted without question. The fact that an event is said to be remembered by someone does not automatically qualify it for the status of history. The evidence which is the memory must come up for the most rigorous examination before the event to which it claims to bear witness is established. That is, while the memory may give a *prima facie* authentication to the event which it remembers, the memory itself must be authenticated, and the veracity of the person whose it is. Too easy an identification of history with memory does not do justice to the immense complexity of historical analysis and method.

(iii) Nor is this account of the matter satisfactory, even if we refine it and say that "history consists of things worthy to be remembered", for two reasons. On the one hand, in order to be remembered at all they must have an existence of their own independent of the fact that they are remembered, and it is this kind of existence which gives them status as history rather than the fact that they are remembered. On the other hand, in saying that history consists of things worthy to be remembered, we have only solved one question by raising others, viz. why are they worthy to be remembered? What is the criterion of worth that is here so important? Does every age regard the same things as worthy? In fact, even on the vaguest nodding acquaintance with historical evidence, we can see that a good many things have been remembered that are not worth remembering, and that an even greater number of things have been forgotten that would have been of inestimable benefit to historical research.

The relation of memory to history is not then one of simple identification. The way for the description of the relation may be prepared if we draw a distinction between (a) the memory of individual persons who act in history, and (b) the store of memories, historical evidence in manuscripts, monuments, etc. which are the memory of no single person but rather of the race or nation or community. The relation of memory to history is slightly different according to which of these two notions of memory we have in mind. Both are relevant to our present purpose.

(a) Professor Niebuhr has both of these notions in mind when he deals (pp. 20 ff.) with memory and history, but it is more particularly of the former that he is thinking when he says that "memory represents man's capacity to rise above, even while he is within the temporal flux" (p. 20). I should say that this point must be fully emphasised, for otherwise the second account of the relation of memory to history is invalidated. It is primarily in relation to his own past which he remembers that a man becomes aware of this transcendence of which Professor Niebuhr speaks, just because he realises that he is not in complete bondage to the present. Having discovered in his own experience of the past through memory a certain transcendence of the present, he can then understand the wider implications of the memory of the race, the nation or the community for the history of these groups. In the same way, because through memory I am aware that my own past does not come upon me with the force of natural necessity, so too in the much wider historical scene, memory becomes "the fulcrum of freedom for man in history" (p. 21).

(b) It is, however, more of the second kind of memory

that we think when we discuss the relation of memory to history. The relation may be stated as follows: the function of memory in the constitution of history is to mediate the past to the present. Just as the past persists into the present in the form of memory-data, so it is in terms of memory-data that we first apprehend the past. As we have already noted, Professor Niebuhr sees memory as the fulcrum of freedom. But I feel that we must also add that through memory the necessity exercised upon the present by the past is also appreciated. The historical agent, because of his awareness of the events which have led to the formation of the historical situation in which he finds himself, is also conscious that the future does not hold for him an infinite range of possible lines of action any one of which he may choose to follow. His knowledge of the past reveals that because of certain decisions made by his predecessors in this particular situation certain things are forever impossible. Someone with no memory-knowledge of the past might be inclined to feel bound in the present by rigid natural necessity; but another kind of person—and history has not been lacking in idealists of this sort—might be induced to believe that the whole world lay at his feet, and that all that was required to put momentous changes in train was a free and utterly undetermined act of his will. If, then, we say that memory is the fulcrum of freedom in history, I think that we ought to add that it is also the vehicle of necessity. Such a view would be more in line with our previous analysis of the categories of history, and particularly with the description of the relation of freedom to necessity. Besides, since we have already said that the function of memory is to mediate the past to the present, then we cannot isolate one category from the others and hold that it alone is mediated. It would be wrong, also, to neglect the mass of information, of moral standards, of accumulated wisdom of the race, or experience gained at a dear price, of ideals and values, of rules-of-thumb, of skills and techniques, that is conveyed to the present by memory of the past; and to underestimate the effect of this mass upon the constituting of history in every age. But for the Christian, this category of memory is of supreme importance, for not only does he find himself within the community of the Church

H

which carries within itself a vast mass of the kind just mentioned, but more particularly it is ultimately through the mediation of memory that he comes to know of the great *kairoi* through which his faith is created. The Bible is the Old and the New Israel's memory of these *kairoi*, and such is the Christian economy of salvation that it is only ultimately through hearing the story of these *kairoi* that the individual comes to his own *kairos*.

CHAPTER NINE

HISTORY AND STRUCTURES

To my mind one of the chief values of a doctrine of history which analyses the categories constitutive of history lies in the assistance which it gives us in dealing with three questions: (1) the structural nature of history; (2) the selections that are made from time to time from the different categories by various writers; and (3) the relations between the categories.

(1) A careful analysis of the writing of Butterfield will, I think, show that in addition to describing several of the categories which we have above discussed, he discerns what we might call three structures within history, these structures being constituted of one or more of the categories. The first is the kind of structure with which the ordinary practising historian deals, the historian who, like every other scientist, confines himself to secondary causes and puts aside any presuppositions about a Prime Cause acting in history. The second is referred to by Butterfield when he says (*History and Human Relations*, p. 70) that an interpretation of history is a thesis concerning the organisation of that whole system of necessity in which human beings at any time and period are not imprisoned but more or less involved. The philosopher of history looks for more comprehensive patterns than the practising historian thinks necessary for the understanding of what happens in history. Butterfield's own discrimination of partial judgments upon selfishness and idolatry in secular history is a very good example of this second kind of structural analysis; cf. Marx. But there is the third structure which the Christian describes and of which Butterfield is also conscious, a kind of pattern of Divine acts, which do not come within the purview of those who confine themselves to the first two structures. God's mighty acts in relation to Israel, and supremely His Revelation of Himself in Jesus Christ, would belong to this group.

(2) These several groupings of different categories, all of

which in my opinion co-exist both for the constitution and for the description of history, however, when taken separately, as they so often are, "make sense" of history. If you like, each has an adequate degree of self-sufficiency to justify those who favour it in employing it to the exclusion of the others, or, as so often happens, in attempting to reduce the others to that particular one which they favour. This fact is all too often forgotten by Christians who claim that their interpretation of history is the only one which "makes sense" of history. The apologetic task of the Christian would be greatly reduced in its difficulty if this were the case. The inability of the non-Christian to accept the Christian interpretation is not simply due to his love for the lie instead of the truth, but rather to the fact that he really thinks that he has the truth himself. Each of the structures is therefore a selection from a complex whole, and selection is made by ignoring the categories which form the other structures. We can readily see how this tendency to ignore categories other than those belonging to the specially favoured structure operates in relation to, say, the Marxist interpretation of history, or even to that given by Vico. What we do not always realise is that the same thing is done by those who try to make *Heilsgeschichte* the whole of the Christian interpretation of history. With the latter, there is to be found sometimes a disregard of the fixed nature of the time-process (for example, the affirmation that the Laws were given on Sinai immediately after the Exodus, even though it could not be disproved that the Laws as we have them only grew up gradually over a very long period, an affirmation that was made because the close association of the giving of the Laws with God's gracious act in the Exodus provided a better basis for morality and religion in Israel) and also a disregard of the category of freedom and the place which faith and the community occupy in the *kairoi*. In this form *Heilsgeschichte* is to be understood as the "story of salvation", told out of relation to, or in abstraction from, certain other categories which constitute history. Those who employ this story should be very careful when they add, as they so often do, that "God acts in history"; for then they shall require to redefine the word history in their sentence to allow for their dispensing with those other categories that are normally associated with history. Otherwise, they will run the oft-quoted risk of having more *Heil* than *Geschichte*. This danger arises, I should say, primarily because the *Heilsgeschichte* theorists have endeavoured to convert a recital of the mighty acts of God, which was originally intended for didactic, liturgical, ethical and religious purposes, into something quite foreign to it, namely, an interpretation of history.

That the structures "make sense" in relative isolation from each other is a matter that need not surprise us greatly, for an analogous situation exists in other fields of enquiry. For example, in the problem of the relation of body and mind, the materialist can make a fairly good case for the view that all the physical changes in the body can be accounted for in terms of physical and chemical laws without the postulation of a non-material entity called the "mind"; in fact, he would go further and say that there is simply no evidence for the existence of the mind which cannot be reduced to the clearest physical terms. A subjective idealist for whom matter, including his own body, is only an idea in the mind, has a system that is completely closed. For both materialist and idealist, the order of reality which he affirms is self-sufficient and complete, as you very soon discover if you try to engage either in an argument. Nor is there anything quite so finally frustrating as a discussion with a solipsist, who denies the existence of other selves, and insists on regarding you as one of his own more recalcitrant ideas. There is too much nonsense in the world that "makes sense" for us to take too seriously any theory or system that rests its claim to truth on the fact that it makes sense. But there are other more serious areas in which the structures of which we have been speaking make sense independently of each other. The humanist can see no contradiction in drawing a completely human picture of Jesus Christ; or in describing human virtue in terms that neglect the grace of God. The Zwinglian feels no obligation to accept transubstantiationist or consubstantiationist theories to state what he believes happens in the Sacrament of the Lord's Supper.

It is this relative independence of the structures of each other which makes it possible for different people to accept one in isolation from the rest, and so difficult for them to argue conclusively against each other. At the same time it makes it all the more necessary for us to arrive at some kind of figure or description which enables us best to see how they can be at once related to each other, have significance for each other, and yet retain their independence.

(3) The description which has seemed to me to be most useful is that which employs the concept of dimensions. A dimensional metaphysic has been worked out by the late Professor Daniel Lamont (*Christ and the World of Thought*) in a field allied to that which we are at present studying, namely, our knowledge of the world, other selves and God. The system of relatedness in which I stand to the world around me is the I-It dimension, and the lowest of all. It is the subject-object dimension. The next consists of my relations to other selves —the I-Thou dimension, or subject-subject dimension. The highest of all is the I-God dimension, or the subject-Subject dimension. What I am suggesting is that the three structures which we found in Butterfield's description of history and which we here in effect accept are related to each other in terms of dimensions, and that the dimensional description enables us to determine the relations in which the three structures stand to each other. For dimensions have three specific characteristics —independence, inclusiveness and finally paradox. The independence of the three dimensions or structures we have already discussed at length, and we need not delay further over this characteristic of them.

By inclusiveness we mean that the higher dimension always includes the lower, so that relations that hold on the lower may also hold on the higher, but that on the higher there exist relations that could not exist on the lower. This point can be fairly easily exemplified from geometry (Euclidean). In the personalist dimensional metaphysic from which we began, we can see how the I-God dimension includes the other two, for my relation to my fellow men and to the created world around me, is of great importance to me now that I stand in the new relation to God. In fact, another implication of this characteristic of inclusiveness is that the lower dimensions are enriched when they are included in the higher. Because I am related to God I find suggested to me a whole new range of possible relations to my fellow men and to the created order. I see my fellow men as brethren for whom Christ died, as united with me in a common fellowship of the Church and of the service of God and the world; I see the natural world as the Creation of God, as a Sacrament of His Love, as the vehicle of His Providence, and my attitude to it must be one not of exploitation but of stewardship. So too, I believe, each of the higher structures which we have discovered in history includes the lower. In fact, to take either of the higher in isolation from the lower produces a false abstraction and a formality which does not do sufficient justice to the full content of history. Thus we do not describe the Incarnation at all adequately if we do not mention the ordinary details with which the technical practising historian deals. "And it came to pass in those days that there went out a decree from Caesar Augustus, that all the world should be taxed" (Lk. 2.1). Nor does Providence have any content except in terms of "the mercies that are new every morning", nor the freedom of faith other than in terms of *kairoi* which occur in the lives of men and women, in the midst of the socio-economic and political complexities of their own day. But just as the higher structures derive content from the lower, so the lower are enriched by being set in the midst of wider systems of relationship. There were many other decrees about taxation in the Roman Empire, but this particular one of which St. Luke speaks derived its significance from the higher structure into which it had been absorbed. Many men had been crucified under the Emperor, but one Crucifixion was particularly related to the Divine economy of salvation and it could be understood fully only in that wider setting.

The third characteristic of dimensional existence is the paradoxical relation in which the dimensions stand to each other; or, more precisely, the position may be put thus, that relations which hold on any higher dimension appear as paradoxical when viewed from the standpoint of the lower dimension. From the I-It dimension it is paradoxical that on the I-Thou dimension there should be an object which is also a subject and a subject which is also an object; that there should be knowledge of subject by object as well as of object by subject.

In the same way, it is paradoxical for the I-Thou dimension that there should be a Subject who is subject not only for me at this time and in this place, but for countless other people in countless other places; that there should be a Person who knows my own mind and self better than I know them; that this Person should be able to transcend the barriers that separate the human I from the human Thou, so that He is able to dwell within me to inspire me and to enlighten me, from my side of the I-God relationship. Similarly for the technical historian it necessarily appears as a paradox that the destruction of an idolatrous nation should at one and the same time be the result of an attack by another nation and due to the judgment of God; that the crossing of the Red Sea should be simultaneously explicable in terms of certain climatic conditions which were unusual but nevertheless naturally caused, and of the will of God to save a nation that had at the time little to commend it either to God or to its neighbours. Instances could be multiplied in which we referred to many of the paradoxes so frequently employed in modern theology.

(4) The following comments may be made upon this dimensional treatment of the relations of the structures within history to one another:

(a) It will be readily observed that there appears to be a certain incompatibility between the two characteristics of independence and inclusiveness. This apparent incompatibility must be allowed to stand, for it draws attention to certain facts which are of great importance. First, from the human point of view, the integration of the lower structures into the higher, or of the different categories with each other, is a humanly impossible task. Our awareness of the details of occurrence, and much more so of the activities of God, is far too inadequate for us to claim that such integration would ever be possible for us. Secondly, it is only for God in His omniscience that the structures which we so imperfectly discern in history are one. What is fragmentary for us is unitary for Him. Thirdly, the integration which we are by God's grace enabled to discern, particularly at the *kairoi*, yields us such insights into the nature of God and His relation to human history that we are obliged to regard the inclusiveness as predominant over the independence in the final resort. In other words, in the *kairoi* we are given not only the detailed integration of circumscribed sections of the various structures, but a basis for describing in general terms the relations that hold between the structures, even though the details are withheld from us. If the integration that holds at the *kairoi* did not obtain in the other sections of history, then even the *kairoi* would not be what we are given to understand them to be.

(*b*) Just because of the inter-relatedness of the dimensions, the Christian can never rightly disregard the work that goes on at the lower dimensions, nor can he neglect them in his doctrine of history. He will be humble before the thoroughness of the expert, believing that thoroughness is relevant to his own constructions of history. That is, *Heilsgeschichte* is not independent of the results of secular historical analysis. At the same time, and because of the paradoxical relations of the dimensions, the Christian will not accept as final the secular historian's dismissal of the relations that are claimed to exist on the higher dimensions, where categories obtain which he does not know or rejects.

(*c*) Because the Christian is aware of these categories, he is enabled to discern certain structures on the second dimension which the non-Christian cannot discern. These are what Professor Niebuhr would call "tangential meanings", the structures which are sufficiently discernible for a person like A. J. Toynbee to erect a whole philosophy of civilisations upon them, or for Vico to formulate his "universal ideal history". But the Christian's assertions of these "tangential meanings" will be shot through with a scepticism which is not apparent in either Toynbee or Vico, a scepticism bred of his awareness both of the complexity of the historical process and of the fragmentariness of outlook which is all that is attainable by one so involved in history. His knowledge of the higher dimensions —even allowing for this necessary scepticism—leads to two important results in the Christian's search for the tangential meanings. First, it predisposes him to discovering connections and analogies which the purely technical historian will miss. For example, Butterfield's Christian faith obviously is the inspiration of his discovery of the bias to self-interest, "the

gravitational pull", of the partial judgments which he affirms
to occur within history, and of "the history which works over
our heads". Secondly, it affords him a higher vantage point
from which to appraise the judgments made about history
by those who do not share the Christian insights into human
nature and historical process. He may not be able himself to
state unambiguously the absolute truth about any given period
of history but he will be able to detect the pretensions to absolute
truth, the delusions and the false constructions of other interpretations.

(d) While it must be said that the Christian doctrine of
history "makes sense" of history, this statement requires the
gravest qualifications. For at the same time it introduces
profounder depths of meaninglessness into history than any
of the other competing views, and at the following points:

(i) As Butterfield and Professor Niebuhr both argue, because
historical events are in part at least the outcome of the free
decisions of persons, which cannot be resolved into forces,
economic, political and social, that may have been influencing
them at the time of their actions, there must always remain
an element of unknowability in all historical analysis. We can
never fully know what the motives were which actuated the
behaviour of the persons we study, even when we have their
own words as alleged evidence. Any philosophy of history
which deals only with the necessary structures that surround
human action is relieved of the responsibility of dealing with
this residuum of incomprehensibility. So also are those
philosophies which take as their unit of historical process
either whole civilisations or social groups.

(ii) By relating God Himself to history, by taking the
Revelation given in Jesus Christ seriously as relevant to
historical process, by seeing God involved in history, the
Christian doctrine of history creates problems which are not
even imagined on shallower analyses. The tragedy of human
sin is not diminished but greatly increased by the fact of the
Cross; not only is it revealed to us in the Cross that sin is an
uglier thing than men had previously thought it to be, but
sin itself at the Cross expresses itself more viciously than ever
before in human history. The fact that this same sin is also

forgiven through the Cross and that the darkness of Calvary is shattered by the radiance of Easter does not alter the fact that the darkness was really dark, and that there was in that darkness an ultimate meaninglessness. To my mind man's sinful rejection of God's love does not "make sense" to a degree which far surpasses all those other events in life that we so often call meaningless. In other words, the affirmation of the higher dimensions introduces an element of meaninglessness into history and into events that occur on the lower dimensions which does not exist for those whose judgments are based simply on empirical observations made at those lower levels. In relation again to the death of Christ, we can see quite easily that that Death can be given a simple explanation by the technical historian who lists its various causes—the offended dignity of the Pharisees, their fear for their religious authority, the treachery of Judas, the weak will of Pilate, and so on. But set this same event in relation to the Love of God, and to His purpose of Salvation, and a certain incomprehensibility has invaded the situation which all the theories of the Atonement cannot finally dispel.

SHORT BIBLIOGRAPHY

BAILLIE, J. *The Belief in Progress*
BERDYAEV, N., *The Meaning of History*
BUTTERFIELD, H., *Christianity and History*
BUTTERFIELD, H., *History and Human Relations*
COLLINGWOOD, R. G., *The Idea of History*
CROCE, B., *Theory and History of Historiography*
CULLMANN, O., *Christ and Time*
DODD, C. H., *History and the Gospel*
FLINT, R., *History of the Philosophy of History*
GEYL, P., *From Ranke to Toynbee*
GOGARTEN, F., *Demythologising and History*
HODGES, H. A., *The Philosophy of Wilhelm Dilthey*
HOFMANN, J. C. K., *Prophecy and Fulfilment*
LÖWITH, K., *Meaning in History*
MACMURRAY, J., *The Clue to History*
MANDELBAUM, M., *The Problem of Historical Knowledge*
MARSH, J., *The Fulness of Time*
NIEBUHR, R., *Faith and History*
RUST, E. C., *The Christian Understanding of History*
SHINN, R., *Christianity and the Problem of History*
TILLICH, P., *An Interpretation of History*
WOOD, H. G., *Christianity and the Nature of History*

INDEX OF NAMES

INDEX OF SUBJECTS

PRINTED IN GREAT BRITAIN BY
OLIVER AND BOYD LTD.
EDINBURGH